How to Meet Men as Smart as You

Sandee Brawarsky

A Fireside Book
Published by Simon & Schuster
New York London Toronto Sydney Tokyo Singapore

FIRESIDE
Rockefeller Center
1230 Avenue of the Americas
New York, New York 10020

FIRESIDE and colophon are registered trademarks of Simon & Schuster Inc.

Designed by Hyun Joo Kim
Manufactured in the United States of America

1   3   5   7   9   10   8   6   4   2

Library of Congress Cataloging-in-Publication Data

Brawarsky, Sandee.
How to meet men as smart as you / Sandee Brawarsky.
p.   cm.
"A Fireside book."
1. Dating (Social customs) 2. Mate selection. I. Title.
HQ801.B853   1994
646.7'7—dc20   94-12342
CIP
ISBN 0-671-86496-3

Six lines of dialogue from *Fiddler on the Roof* by Joseph Stein. From *Fiddler on the Roof* by Joseph Stein. Copyright © 1964 by Joseph Stein. Reprinted by permission of Crown Publishers, Inc.. *Permissions continued on page 6.*

For my parents,
Muriel and Jack Brawarsky

Contents

	Preface	9
	Introduction: First, Good News	11
1	On Being a Matchmaker	17
2	The First Four Rules	26
3	On Being Matched	30
4	Interesting Places to Meet Interesting Men	38
5	More Great Places to Meet Great Men	58
6	First Words: Flirting With Dignity	80
7	First, Old Friends	86
8	First Phone Calls	89
9	First Dates	98
10	First Things to Do Next	113
11	A Special Note on the Second Time Around	120
12	Overdating: Too Many Men	127
13	Last Dates? Last Words	130
	Acknowledgments	135
	Index	139

Preface

$\mathcal{J}$ love making matches between women and men, but I'm not a bosomy old woman with an oversized satchel who dashes from kitchen to kitchen, enters unannounced, and feasts on tea and gossip. Nor do I advertise my services in newspapers, with a stunning photograph and alluring copy. I charge no fee.

To my friends, I'm an unrelenting matchmaker and I'm also the personal trainer of dating. I hear their best and worst stories, and I offer advice on how to meet terrific and available men. Almost with a sense of mission, I "fix up" lots of couples. When my efforts succeed—that is, when the fixed-up man and woman get along—I'm pleased, proud, and satisfied. Should liking grow to loving and they decide to marry, my joy is uncontained.

One of my greatest accomplishments is that I've introduced six couples who are now happily married (and numbers 7 and 8 look serious) and have eight children among them. At the wedding of couple number 6, three women followed me into the ladies' room and, pressing their business cards into my hand, asked me to do something for them. This book is for them.

Introduction

First, Good News

Love does not make the world go round,
looking for it does.
> —Charlie, in Herb Gardner's
> *Conversations With My Father*

In some cultures, women don't have to worry about meeting men because marital decisions are made for them. Parents might promise their infants in marriage at birth, or wait until they reach their teen years to begin negotiating for a spouse.

No doubt people can find great happiness in such situations, but I feel fortunate to be part of a culture that leaves the decisions about relationships to the individual. I cherish freedom of choice. That brings us to dating—one of the ways we exercise our independence in matters of the heart. But freedom doesn't make life easy. Meeting potential romantic partners is a challenge; it's also an acquired skill.

I know lots of wonderful and available women who lament not finding anyone decent to go out with. They are bright and energetic and successful in most facets of their lives—but they feel blue over their dateless state. My hope is to help them not only find dates but meet lots of men as smart as they are.

A *Brides* magazine survey found that 80 percent of single men wish they were married. They're wishing they'd met *you*. All those studies that claim women over a certain age have an unlikely chance of getting married are not statistically accurate—and simply not true.

Whatever your age and wherever you live, you have much cause for optimism. There are lots of single men out there (38 million, and that's just in the United States), and no doubt many would be honored, delighted, ecstatic to meet you, if only they had the chance.

This book is about creating those chances. Finding a smart man isn't about statistics; it's mostly about timing—being ready at the time your path crosses that of a man also at the right stage of his life. It's about developing opportunities for yourself. After all, the more paths you travel, the greater the prospects for interesting intersections.

On Fate, Destiny, Karma— and *Achieving* Good Luck

Perhaps you believe that there is someone out there who is perfect for you, a man whose heart and yours fit together like two halves of a whole. You know that your destiny is to meet him. This is a fabulous romantic notion—but it's still up to you to hasten destiny. It would be nice if he were just to show up on your doorstep one day. But it's unlikely that he will.

Maybe your sense of how the world works is more in line with my grandmother's pragmatic notion that "every pot has a cover." Several covers could fit, and you'll choose the one that fits best for you. It's up to you to go out and meet as many as you can.

A friend who has a beautiful garden lined with pecan trees reminds me that there are two methods for nut gathering. You can collect those that fall in their time each day. But if you can climb up the tree and shake it, the pecans fall like rain, and piles of them will surround you.

What do halves and wholes, pots and covers, and pecan trees have to do with dating? Whether you believe in love as destiny or not, you'd be wise to shake the tree and gather its gifts.

In order to meet interesting men, you'll need to take action. It's not always easy to begin a conversation, go on a blind date (let alone your ninetieth), or call him back, but it's worthwhile and ultimately rewarding. You can have some fun, and enjoy the many prospects you'll encounter.

Your All-Inclusive Guide to Dating

Well-meaning friends will advise you to get out there and meet people. You might be wondering where, exactly, "there" is. The truth is, it's different for each woman. The advice in these pages will help you find your own way and beyond. There are routines you can master to encourage your friends to really assist you in meeting men and choices of the best places to go and things to do.

You'll find both familiar and novel plans of action, and some ideas you may have considered but weren't certain how to execute. You'll also discover the inside track on matchmaking. With smart advice on everything from first encounters to first dates (and how to move ahead when you want to) and everything in between, from solo vacations, jury duty, chance meetings, personal ads, and computer networking to blind dates, fax dates, romantic friendships, post-divorce dates, and dating burnout, you'll become a dating virtuoso. All this expertise might well lead you into happy retirement from dating.

Think of this book as a menu of strategies. Read everything, decide what's most appealing to you, and try it. Even better, make efforts in several directions at once. Try courses of action that are entirely new, attempt things you can barely picture yourself doing. Go for it. At its worst, dating is great for providing laughs, and at its best, you might find more happiness than you can imagine.

Some Wise and Street-Smart Advice

The most valuable recommendation of all is about attitude: Understand wholeheartedly that possibilities loom everywhere. You never know what circumstances can lead to meeting new people.

After being mugged a few years ago, I had to walk around with a bandage over my broken nose, complementing my newly chipped front tooth. The white tape holding the bandage in place extended from cheek to cheek. I looked like I was in bad shape. But during that period, I set a personal record for having the most men—practically strangers—ask me to go out with them. The detective working on my case wanted to take me to dinner; the locksmith who changed the locks on my doors left his number everywhere and asked that I call him when I felt up to going for a drive; there were others too. I joked with friends about marketing a facial bandage to single women as a tool for finding dates.

All that attention had to do with sympathy, curiosity ("What happened to you?"), and what became a conversation starter. I'm not advocating getting mugged as a way to meet smart men. But I believe that a sense of humor and an open attitude can turn any situation into one of promise. Happy endings can unfold from all sorts of beginnings.

If this book has a mantra, it's this: Be open to possibility. Remember that you have good reason to be upbeat, confident, and hopeful. And be ready to recognize a great opportunity when it appears.

And, although this is obvious advice, understand that for your efforts to be effective, you truly have to want—and feel ready—to meet new people.

This is the point where I'd better admit to being single. Yes, I have a string of success stories as a matchmaker and I continue to make matches with enthusiasm and ease. And, yes, I've never been married. So why am I giving advice about how to meet men? Because I've been there; I've been in your shoes and I'm still dancing in them. I make matches (I'll tell you more about how it's done later on) and I've been matched—to varying degrees of success—many times. I haven't officially checked, but I might hold the world record for going on more first dates than any other woman in America. Many of them have been coffee dates—sitting and chatting and asking getting-acquainted questions over cappuccino, whether in sidewalk cafés, company cafeterias, hotel coffee shops, or local diners. I've managed to meet a lot of smart men that I've been quite fond of—some of whom I've thought about marrying and others whom I've introduced to women they've subsequently married—but I haven't chosen to marry any, yet.

I love single life. That's not to say that I advocate never changing my status. But there's no great hurry at any age. Time clocks? Well, there are biological realities, but we're fortunate to live in an age where there are new technologies, new advances, new options. The race to the altar doesn't have to be fueled by baby fever. Relax and enjoy singlehood while it lasts. Luxuriate in the quiet of your home—or in the noise that you create and control. There's a certain comfort in finding everything as you left it. You don't have to entertain anyone else's relatives. You can go out every night—or not.

If you want to spend those nights out with new and interesting companions, read on.

▲▲

Bookstores across the country now have sections devoted to inspirational books. Meditations for people who eat too much, sleep too much; for the aging, the recovering, the life-changing. If there were a book for the smart single woman . . .

Meditations for Single Women

I enjoy being single. My life feels full, and I value that. I'm blessed with great friends, and I cherish the time I spend with them. It would be nice to have a man I care about in my life right now, but without one I'm doing just fine. I don't need to be with a man to be happy.

I know that I'll find a man I love. When it happens, I'll be ready.

I promise not to put my life on hold because I'm single. I deserve to do those things I enjoy doing *now*. There's no reason not to plan fabulous vacations, dine in restaurants with friends, decorate my home, talk to a financial advisor about my future. My future has already begun.

At least I'm not unhappily married. At least I'm not plotting to murder my husband.

▼▼

On Being a Matchmaker

Life is a romantic business.
　　　　　　—Justice Oliver Wendell Holmes

Love is like playing checkers. You have to know which man to move.
　　　　　　—Jackie "Moms" Mabley

I define my role as matchmaker as someone who jump-starts romance for others. I arrange dates, not necessarily marriages. I take great satisfaction when my matches become marriages, but once I've introduced a couple, I let them decide where the relationship will go.

Since the days of one of the earliest recorded matchmakers—the biblical Eliezer, who selected Rebeccah as a wife for Isaac—the profession has provided a vital service. A Moscow-based matchmaker who recently set up shop told *The Wall Street Jour-*

nal that "this business won't die. It will go on forever. Like hair-cutting." Louis Rubin, a New York matchmaker, is said to have arranged over seven thousand marriages by the end of his career in the early part of this century. But it's not easy work. According to a Yiddish proverb, "Making matches is a task as difficult as dividing the Red Sea."

Many who shared my trade over the ages saw their labor as unrelated to love; in fact, the business of finding a mate was deemed too important to be left to something as capricious as love. Some contemporary matchmakers would concur; for them, bringing together couples is a version of a high-powered merger and acquisition. Not me. I make introductions where I see potential for mutual attraction, shared values, camaraderie—and yes, love.

When you think of matchmakers, the person likely to come to mind is Yente from the Broadway show and movie *Fiddler on the Roof.* Yente was the classic type: legendary for loquaciousness and the tendency to exaggerate certain qualities and gloss over deficiencies in describing potential partners. Love wasn't her concern. As she would have gladly told you, she had enough to worry about without concerning herself with love.

There are matchmakers and there are matchmakers. You'll find many listed in the telephone book; some are so talented they seem clairvoyant; others are unexceptional. There are the part-time practitioners, no less astute and enthusiastic than the professionals: people like me who simply have a habit of using every opportunity to launch blind dates. Although I make matches with care and professionalism, I do it for fun, not livelihood. I enjoy making connections between people; I agree with Yente: "It gives me satisfaction to make people happy—what better satisfaction is there?"

You might think that the only people who would resort to using matchmakers are people who are so "romantically challenged" that they'd never be able to find a date for themselves. Wrong. Lots of terrific couples—including some you must know—meet though blind dates. Behind each of those matches is the design of a matchmaker or a caring friend or relative moonlighting as one.

▲▲

Yente: Avram, I have a perfect match for your son. A wonderful girl.

Avram: Who is it?

Yente: Ruchel, the shoemaker's daughter.

Avram: Ruchel? But she can hardly see. She's almost blind.

Yente: Tell the truth, Avram, is your son so much to look at? The way she sees and the way he looks, it's a perfect match.

—from *Fiddler on the Roof*
by Joseph Stein

▼▼

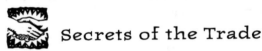 Secrets of the Trade

Although there's much to be learned from Yente's insights and those of my many wise predecessors, I try to be more particular and not look at matchmaking as some kind of business transaction. Also, I believe in full disclosure at the beginning to all parties involved. While it's not necessary to divulge someone's college grade-point average, I wouldn't describe a 350-pound man as "somewhat broad-shouldered."

My "clients" are friends, although I occasionally get calls from people I don't know who've heard that I match people. I've even gotten calls from mothers calling on behalf of (but unbeknownst to) their kids. If I don't know the person well, I try to meet him or her first and ascertain if there's a real interest in meeting someone. I try to avoid situations where a person's only motivation for being introduced is to satisfy his or her parents.

The downside of being a matchmaker is dealing with disappointment. Often I'm more disappointed than the couple when a match that seemed perfect fizzles. More painful, though, is the disappointment when one party is very interested and the other isn't, and the former wants advice in drawing out or re-connecting with the other. My rule is not to get involved at that point, and I try to make that clear at the beginning. I'll do everything I can to initiate the first date, but after that my work is done. Of course, I love to hear about first impressions, but I usually resist the urge to check in, assuming that when things are pleasant (or better), I'll hear about it.

I'm not only bringing people together for romance; my matchmaking instincts carry over into everything I do. I have introduced several groupings of friends who became apartment mates and helped others find apartments, and I've connected many people with new jobs or freelance projects. I've been the go-between on many occasions between writers and literary agents, patients and doctors, my shoemaker and lots of new clients, parents of similar-aged children with each other, and potential partners in tennis and bridge.

Matchmaking Methodology and Manners

You probably wouldn't think twice about helping a talented friend land a new job. So why not do everything you can to help her find someone to go out with? She may be able to return the favor for you.

I encourage everyone, particularly people who'd like to be matched, to try being a matchmaker for others. Many women have male friends they care about but wouldn't date—for a range of reasons—but they can introduce these guys to appropriate women. You never know.

Here's some practical advice about my matchmaking system, in case you want to experiment. I collect people—or rather, their names. The first people I think about are my friends, colleagues, acquaintances. I never take for granted that various people I know know one another. There are many possible introductions to be made even within your own group of friends. One man and woman I brought together ten years ago—and are now married—knew each other but never thought to date until I suggested it. They thank me whenever they see me.

When I meet new people who are appealing, I look for clues as to whether they're single—rings, questions answered in the "we" form, or a spouse who cuts in on the conversation. There are creative ways to find out someone's marital status. A seventy-two-year-old happily married man was puzzled when a woman on the next tennis court came up to him as he was leaving and asked if his wife played bridge. Although he was confused, it's clear that what she was really asking was whether he had a wife.

If I'm fairly certain that a person is unattached, I ask if he or she would like to be fixed up, quickly making a joke about my impressive track record. I try to get a sense of his or her personality, background, and interests, and immediately start thinking of possibilities. Once I did introduce a man and woman who weren't exactly unattached. Each was talking about ending relationships that were going nowhere—and each expressed interest in meeting someone new. They're now happily attached—married, in fact—to each other.

I'm lucky to have a good memory for details, which helps. It's as though I fill out an index card on everyone eligible I speak with and add the cards, with a photo attached, to a giant Rolodex. When I come up with two people that seem to match, I let the idea percolate for a few days before acting on it.

(For those who want to try out the system and choose not to store all of this information in their heads, a package of index cards will work. If you don't have a great memory, it's also a good idea to note on the card any dates that you do arrange, so that if you come up with an idea for the second time—brilliant as it may seem—you don't fix up the same couple twice. That might call into question your credentials.)

The inspiration for a particular match may have to do with a shared skill in sailing or interest in Renaissance art, similar Midwest or suburban backgrounds, identical bohemian or buttondown styles of dressing, or kindred values and goals. Sometimes I'm struck by a complementary quality—she loves to drive and he has a terrific sense of direction but never passed his road test. Or I have an impulse, not necessarily rational, that a certain couple will click. It might even be something about their voices. I have no theory as to what is the most reliable predictor of success; my choices are good guesses, based on some instinctive feeling, and when they're right they seem brilliant. I get it less right some of the time too. Sometimes when my guesses are wrong, the parties tell me that they understand what I was thinking, but it just didn't work. Most important, I keep trying.

▲▲

(Two women are talking off to the side at a wedding)

Rita: I know the perfect guy for you.

Babs: Who?

Rita: He's brilliant. He's attractive.

Babs: Well, who is it? What? There's a hitch. I'm waiting.

Rita: He's in prison.

Babs: Rita, I would say that's a drawback.

Rita: Nothing terrible. Insider trading. He made a fortune in the market and he'll be out soon. A couple of years.

Babs: You mean with good behavior?

—from *Crimes and Misdemeanors*
by Woody Allen

▼▼

There's an optimum way of setting the idea for a first date into motion. I try to check with the man first; I tell him a little about the woman I have in mind, and if he's interested, I tell him I'll check with her—assuring him that she'll be interested—and then get back to him with her number. Before I approach the woman, I like to have a commitment from the man that he'll follow up and call. When I contact the woman, I similarly give her a brief description of the man, and I want to be sure that there wasn't prior contact—that she didn't date his brother, or work with him—that would make their meeting uncomfortable. I tell her to expect his call. It's essential that she knows that he'll be calling. Making that first call can be difficult enough without being greeted with *"Who?* I never heard anything about you. *Why* are you calling?" After giving the woman the man's name, I call him with her office or home phone number, whichever she prefers. Then, I step back.

I use my best efforts to follow this system, as it seems to allow the least chance for disappointment—an expected phone call that never arrives, or a rejection on the first call.

Sometimes there's neither time nor opportunity for all that checking. Sometimes the man will call the woman immediately, before I've been able to do some preliminaries. And sometimes the woman will make the first phone call. Nothing wrong with that.

I recently asked a woman I know who enjoys making matches ("My only requirement is that they invite me to the wedding") about her methods. A widow in her sixties, she first finds a man "who's willing to accept a phone number and knows what to do with it" and then links him with an age- and religion-appropriate women "who's willing to give it a shot." No more logistics than that. As she finished explaining, she turned and asked me if I knew anyone for her. Although I didn't at the moment, she's on my list. You never know.

Collaborative Matchmaking

I'm always curious to know whether friends and colleagues have single friends, brothers, or brothers-in-law. I ask them directly, and gather the names and whatever other information I can. Then, I ask the people I know to check with the people they know if they are open to being introduced to someone. I like to think of this as teamwork. What gets complicated is that my connections have to tell their connections that they don't know the intended date, but that they trust my judgment 100 percent and think the person sounds great.

I've even done this successfully with three people in the middle; that is, I (B) asked a friend (C) to ask a friend of hers (D) about her son's (E) interest in meeting a cousin of mine (A). So, C, who was the real force in making this match happen, knew B and D quite well, but had never met A or E. (This sounds complicated, but bear with me.) C had plenty of faith in B's and D's opinions, and A and E trusted B and C, respectively, and after several phone calls up and down this chain, A and E met and each was quite pleased (and so were B, C, and D).

Certain people are reluctant to get involved in matchmaking because they see it as meddling, and I try to convince them that they're not interfering but doing good work in the world by helping to connect people who really *would* like to meet. If they're not convinced, I try again, then look elsewhere for resources.

Clandestine Matchmaking

Yes, I admit that I sometimes arrange matches without telling either the man or woman or both. When I know people are reluctant to date, I've invited them to parties and dinners along with a potential match. I try to orchestrate seating arrangements and some conversation, but whatever happens—or doesn't—is out of my control. I'm pleased to report that two contented married couples met at my kitchen table. Another couple met when I invited him to a concert where she was performing. Although I've had some striking successes using covert means—and I continue such plotting—I prefer the straightforward method of matchmaking.

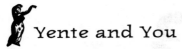

Yente and You

So go on, a matchmaker you too can be. Once you try it, you may find that the effort becomes second nature. A success story will hook you for life.

Making matches for your friends also can be a gracious way of getting out of a second date (see page 117). You can also be your own matchmaker. If there's someone you know from a distance, find someone who knows him and ask to be introduced. After all, you're doing that man a favor.

In *The Matchmaker*, a Thornton Wilder play that opened on Broadway in 1955, the title character, Mrs. Dolly Gallagher Levi (played by Ruth Gordon in the original production, which was the inspiration for *Hello Dolly*), describes herself as "a woman who arranges things." Hired by a wealthy merchant to find him a wife, Mrs. Levi accomplishes the mission: She marries him.

The First Four Rules

Never let the other fellow set the agenda.
> —James Baker, former
> U.S. Secretary of State

There is very little difference between men and women in space.
> —Helen Sharman,
> British astronaut

*L*ooking for a man isn't unlike searching for a job. There may be a recession, but there are still great opportunities, if you look in the right places. Tom Loftus, an outplacement counselor who helps individuals reassess their skills to reenter the job market, shared the following four rules for landing the job you want:

1. You're in control.
2. Talk to everyone.

3. Everything is negotiable.
4. Don't turn anything down before it's offered.

I've learned that these can be rules for life—and they can certainly aid in finding men to date as well as finding a job.

You're in Control

You're chief of protocol. You make the rules. You decide when you're ready to date and who to go out with. You decide if you don't want to go or don't want to go see him again. You determine how fast, which direction. Not to say that serendipity and Cupid and well-intentioned friends can't play a role, but ultimately you're in charge of how you respond to chance, fate, and your best friend from high school who has a brother-in-law. You're director, producer, stage manager, and star—at least at this point. Later on, once the show is on the road, you'll have to share decision making with your costar.

Talk to Everyone

Even if you dislike using the word *network* as a verb, that's the first action you'll need to take: Tell lots of people you know—colleagues at work, relatives you like, tennis partners, your ophthalmologist, the person who teaches your computer skills workshop—that you'd like their help in something important. Ask your college roommate to talk to her husband, your neighbor to think about her clients. Say something like: "I have a favor to ask. I've decided that I really want to meet an interesting man this summer [fall/winter/spring] and I know that you know lots of people. I wonder if you'd keep me in mind if you run into anyone who might be appropriate. I'd be really grateful." (And to single friends add: "I'd be happy to do the same for you.") You may feel as if you have to make some apologies at the beginning or declare your embarrassment up front. Don't.

Be honest and straightforward, and you'll be heard. If they ask you what kind of person you're looking for, give a brief answer in terms of age, life situation, and anything that's critical to you. But don't sound too definitive about a certain type, and if they don't ask the question, don't offer an answer. Be open to any possibility, at least for now. There'll be lots of time to be discriminating later on.

▲▲▲

Advice from Celluloid Dates

1. *When Harry Met Sally* (Here's inspiration to finally date the man you've been pals with for years.)
2. *Crossing Delancey* (Listen to your grandmother.)
3. *The Cemetery Club* (You can meet an interesting man anywhere.)
4. *Husbands and Wives* (There is dating after marriage. Be careful about matching your friend with a man you'd like to date.)
5. *Defending Your Life* (Flirting continues in heaven.)
6. *Sleepless in Seattle* (Follow your fantasy.)

▼▼

Everything Is Negotiable

Try to keep in mind that even though you've always assumed you'd fall in love with someone who shares your passion for old movies, you may discover that you enjoy the company of an opera buff who doesn't own a VCR. One can negotiate evenings at the opera and evenings watching television. Likewise, country/city, open windows/closed windows, dying to have a large family/hate children, early riser/late sleeper, tofu and brown rice/steak and potatoes, love visiting relatives/can't live far enough away, and other differences might be negotiable—or at any rate, they shouldn't be grounds for dismissal in the beginning. People determined not to have children sometimes become happy parents. Even people who alphabetize their spices can adapt, or your feelings about a potential partner can be transformed from contempt to acceptance. Differences can ultimately keep people apart, but sometimes those lines of distinction just make things interesting and aren't necessarily obstacles. You may find that you'll simply agree to disagree or find a satisfactory compromise. What drove you crazy in another relationship may have little effect now, at a different time, in a different setting, with a new person. As Pulitzer prize–winning playwright Wendy Wasserstein once said, "Life is a negotiation."

Don't Turn Anything Down Before It's Offered

Welcome all possibilities. Don't decide that you won't go out with someone before he has called. And don't decide you won't marry him on the basis of that first telephone conversation. There can be lots of surprises. Say yes first. You'll have the option to say no later on.

To clobber you on the head with this message one more time: Try not to prejudge; be open. There will be plenty of time for negotiation.

On Being Matched

You look, you meet, you try, you see. Sometimes it fits, sometimes it doesn't.
> —Mrs. Mandlebaum, the
> matchmaker in *Crossing
> Delancey*

Tact is after all a kind of mind reading.
> —Sarah Orne Jewett

*S*ay yes. A friend calls and asks if you'd be interested in meeting her brother's law partner. You have nothing to lose but an hour of your time—and a whole lot to gain. Remember that you can design the scenario. Have your friend give her friend your telephone number. When he calls, suggest that you get together for coffee or a drink. Your first meeting can be brief, but just in case, clear additional time afterward. That way, you can escape after forty-five minutes if his conversation is putting you to sleep or, on the positive side, if things are going well you have the possibility of extending drinks to dinner. (See Chapter 9 for some suggested venues for blind dates.)

Certain friends may prefer the "group blind date" approach. They'll want to be present for the introductions, and might suggest a dinner party or a group outing the first time you encounter the man they have in mind for you. Some such hosts are less subtle than others. ("I can already tell that you two make a fabulous couple.") It's usually preferable to meet the person in a one-on-one situation, when you're not being watched and the potential match isn't under close scrutiny by your well-meaning friends. But if they insist on a group event—or assert that their male friend is more comfortable that way—go along with their plans, at least once. You might find, as some women do, that there's less pressure when there are other people around. If you find the man interesting, you can arrange some private time later on. Then, on your first real date with him, you might feel more like you're dating someone you already know.

Blind dates aren't so blind after all. Someone you know has an inkling that you might like someone else they know. Those inklings can be powerful. Another great thing about blind dates is that men are more likely to arrive on time, make a real effort to make the evening go smoothly, be polite—in short, be on their best behavior—because they feel like your mutual friend is a witness. And you both know there will be phone discussions about the date the next day.

Some generous friends will organize blind dates or matches for you without being asked. Other people you know, no less generous but in need of some coaxing, may be great resources too. They're likely to be flattered that you think well enough of them to ask. If people are hesitant, be sure they understand that you won't hold them responsible if things don't work out.

Once asked, most people enjoy the challenge of fixing up their friends and acquaintances. They'll even start asking their other friends, relatives, and associates if they know any great single men. You needn't be wary if your matchmaker doesn't know the other party directly. There usually is some connection, so suspend your skepticism. Again, you have everything to gain.

Be sure to graciously thank all of your matchmakers—even if you can't figure out why on earth they thought you would like their friend. They meant well. If they missed, let them know if it was a near-miss or a way-off-miss, and encourage them to try again.

Remember, talk to everyone. Your reach is further than your immediate vision. Think of *Six Degrees of Separation:* You're only six people away from just about anyone in the world you might want to meet. Here are some people you shouldn't overlook recruiting into your circle of matchmakers.

☑ Real Estate Agents

They're among the first to encounter people relocating to a new city or suburb, or moving to a different part of town. They also know about men who are newly single, moving into their own place, and others who buy or rent vacation homes as singles. Good agents have to be good judges of character, reliability, and solvency. Since they're familiar with matching people with spaces, dreams, and realistic expectations, introducing men and women should be a natural skill.

☑ Priests, Ministers, Rabbis, Imams, Other Religious Leaders

They also have inside information about eligible men, and often good insights and can make wise choices about people. By nature of their profession, they can be trusted to be discreet and honest. Religious figures can be particularly helpful in connecting people from similar backgrounds.

☑ Lawyers, Accountants

Anyone who provides professional services has an ever-growing list of clients, among whom there might be some potential dates for you. Those who work in partnerships or firms might also think about interesting colleagues and associates.

☑ Architects, Interior Designers

Like real estate agents, they're privy to important facts about transitions in people's living arrangements. You can ask these professionals if they've done work for eligible men you might want to meet, and if so, they're likely to cooperate in arranging for you to see the beautifully designed space—while the client is at home.

▲▲

A friend writes: I was more excited than usual about a certain blind date. A gym friend gave my phone number to a colleague. We had a lively telephone conversation where we determined that we had lots in common, and we made a plan to have dinner a few nights later at a lovely restaurant he selected. We described what we looked like so that we'd recognize each other. When I arrived, I was searching the bar area for a tall man with a beard. There was only one bearded man, and I approached him. When we looked at each other, we both remembered at the same moment that we had gone on a blind date ten years before. To say that earlier evening was dull is an understatement. My enthusiasm disappeared in a flash. We ate quickly, said good-night, and I vowed one thing: Even if I wanted to forget the details of an unpleasant date, I had to remember his name.

▼▼

✓ Teachers, Professors

If you keep in touch with your teachers from your past or present schooling, ask them if they know anyone you might like to meet. They may enjoy weaving their own network of contacts closer together.

✓ Salespeople

Friends who work in sales are a terrific resource. Whether in commercial or retail sales, hospital equipment or sporting goods, they come into contact with an amazing variety of people. By training, they have a finely tuned skill of learning what they need to know about their customers' lives. And they love to do favors for their clients. Their instincts aren't solely altruistic; they are courting additional business and hoping their kindness will be returned, but it can't hurt to see what they can do for you.

✓ Hairdressers, Tailors

If your hairdresser or tailor also provides services for men, ask them to scout for potential dates for you when they cut some locks of single hair or adjust the length of single trousers. They have the luxury of chatting with their clients while they perform their jobs, and are always the party in control. Or if you see someone interesting in the shop, ask the professional to intervene on your behalf. Send him or her a new customer in appreciation.

✓ For City Dwellers: Doormen

If you're curious about whether the guy who just moved into 11G is single, your doorman can surely answer the question. The best doormen pride themselves on being discreet, but are usually delighted to assist in your strategizing.

✓ For Suburban and Country Dwellers: Letter Carriers

They know who's who and who's where. Make him or her an ally, and you might hear of interesting new people at new addresses.

▲▲▲

The Nimmonses were married on May 25, 1990, after knowing each other for about five months. Their romance was not conventional, Mrs. Nimmons said. She first met him while he was on Rikers Island [a New York City corrections facility for those awaiting trial] after a friend of hers, also on Rikers, introduced them over the telephone. She became interested in the stranger on the other end of the line. "It was like a blind date," she said.

—*The New York Times*,
December 11, 1992

▼▼▼

✓ Waiters

If you frequent a particular café or restaurant and you befriend the waiters, they'll be quite pleased to introduce you to the man across the room who's sitting alone.

✓ Friends

Enlist all of your friends and relatives to think about the single people with whom they work, play basketball, serve on neighborhood committees, carpool, or attend religious services. They should also comb their pasts for men they went to college with, sang in choir with, learned to sail with, or any old buddies they admire. Ask your newest friends too.

✓ For Single Parents: Your Kids' Friends' Parents

People who have kids will no doubt know of other single parents. Let them know you're open to meeting new people.

✓ Kids

Your kids, whether young or grown up, are likely to have a keen sense of the man they'd like you to meet. Suggest that they keep their eyes and hearts open.

Plan your approaches to these different people when you can spend a quiet and private moment with them. Depending on the nature of your relationship, whether it's a relative, friend, or business contact, you'll need to use varying degrees of diplomacy. Don't be too subtle; speak with candor. You'll find people keen to help. Keep expanding your list of personal matchmakers, and remind them of your request every six months or so. Always promise to return the favor in some way.

▲▲▲

Male Voices

Warren, a San Francisco architect: "I love going on blind dates. It's pretty scary knocking on someone's door and not having any idea, really, who's on the other side. But it's a thrill."

James, a New York realtor: "It's easy. I'm attracted to women who seem interested in meeting me."

Barry, a Boston musician: "Those surveys that talk about how single women outnumber single men are untrue and misleading. It's no easier for men than it is for women to find dates. I could use a guidebook too."

Gene, a Toronto psychologist: "I'm in my forties, and I think it's a myth that men my age are interested only in meeting women in their twenties. I know that a woman who's really interesting to me is going to be closer to my age."

Henry, a London doctor: "I'm drawn to women who have a certain amount of mystery about them. When there's no mystery—whether physical or emotional—I'm not interested."

Norman, a Philadelphia painter: "I look for a sign of inner light, whether through someone's eyes, voice, or gestures. I'm attracted to a quality of aliveness, and I can tell within the first second of meeting someone if they have it. But I realize that I'm not always right."

▼▼

Interesting Places to Meet Interesting Men

I do desire we may be better strangers.
　　　　　—Orlando, in William
　　　　　Shakespeare's *As You Like It*

Fate keeps on happening.
　　　　　—Anita Loos

*C*all it serendipity. My mother met my father at the wedding of a mutual cousin. One of my sisters was offered a lift by her future husband while hitchhiking in Boston; he picked up her and a friend and then joined them at the party where they were headed. My other sister and her husband worked together at a summer camp. And a friend dates a man she went to high school with; they never spoke to one another until they met in a courtroom—on opposite sides of a case—twenty years after graduation.

Like Eve who first glimpsed Adam in the Garden of Eden, most women meet the men they want to marry because they're in the right place at the right time. It may be a stroke of luck, coincidence, a blessing, or a miracle. Even a slip-up, a missed train, a broken heel, or a small chance occurrence can change your life. Being in a certain place and time can turn out to be fruitful for making a new acquaintance.

"Always look nice when you take out the garbage; you never know who you might meet," Jani Blumberg quotes the wisdom of her mother in Wendy Wasserstein's play *Isn't It Romantic*. I don't know of anyone who's met a man either at the trash chute or recycling bins—yet—but Mrs. Blumberg is on the right track. Possibilities lurk in all corners of life.

▲▲

Sophie (With a big, warm smile): Excuse me. Mah name is Sophie Rauschmeyer. Ah just moved into the empty apartment next door. Ah know people in big cities don't usually do this, but Ah promised mah folks Ah would make mah akwaintance with mah neighbors so Ah just want to say it's a pleasure meetin' you and hope Ah see you again. Real soon. 'Bye!

(She gives him a big smile. She turns, closes the door and goes.)

—from *The Star-Spangled Girl*
by Neil Simon

▼▼

Whether meeting a great guy is the result of fate or the ability to let accidents happen or agreeing to meet your accountant's cousin, you increase your chances of being in the right places at the right times by getting yourself to lots of varied places. These include public spaces, events, shops, classes. You need to put yourself in places, activities, and events where you can feel comfortable, confident, and open to possibilities. If you pursue an interest, you're bound to meet people who share that interest, and in that common ground lies the seed of conversation, perhaps a date, even a relationship.

The key is to truly find common ground. Others might encourage you to spend time at hardware stores, shipyards, stock car races, and other sites where men outnumber women. That's good advice only if you enjoy being around hammers and nails, boats, and fast cars. There's no need for you to spend precious hours in places where you have little interest just in the hope of meeting a man. Your time is better spent in activities you know you'll enjoy whether you meet an interesting man or not. (This is not to say that you should avoid hardware stores or other "male" hangouts—on the contrary. While you're debating the benefits of one extension cord over another, be aware of fellow customers. Ask an opinion.)

Keep the principle of "frequent sightings" in mind. If you see someone on a regular basis—whether on the bus, the hallway at work, or anyplace you go to relax—you'll develop a familiarity, and even if you don't speak to one another, you'll soon feel as if you know the person. When you finally have a conversation, it will seem like you're talking to someone you've known for a while, and you might want to see the person with greater frequency.

No doubt you have your own list of favorite places and activities; here are some you might not have considered. Wherever you go, have a pile of your business cards in easy reach.

 BEST PLACES

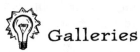 ## Museums
(and Museum Cafés)

A college professor recalls that when he was on army leave in foreign cities, he'd head for the art museum, and would have more success meeting interesting women than his buddies who stuck to the bars. His method was asking women questions (quietly) about the art, and conversation would follow. It's a good idea to notice who is around you as you admire what's on the walls. Don't eliminate the guards as possibilities. Many hold advanced degrees and know a lot about art.

 ## Galleries

As in museums, it's comfortable to be friendly toward people who obviously share one of your interests. Find out the times of openings of new exhibits. Even if you don't know the featured artist whose work is being celebrated (and even if you don't like the art), you'll usually be able to share some wine and conversation with others there.

Auction Houses

Many exhibits of collections and auctions are open to the general public. Like great theater, the proceedings can be full of dramatic moments, outstanding beauty, and intrigue. Arrive early to see what's being sold—and who's buying.

Flea Markets, Crafts Fairs

Enjoy browsing. As you develop an eye for finding objects that appeal to you, broaden your vision to take in the people around you. In these settings, people are often quite friendly; you might chat with those selling, buying, or looking.

Parks, Public Gardens

Wander, sit on a park bench, take in the view. Watch the cyclists and sunbathers (or sled riders) or the power walkers and strollers. Feel free to make conversation with people around you. Find a comfortable spot and read a book; bring a picnic and offer to share some food. Or get a kite and fly it. Feel free to seek advice about getting it aloft or untangled; others will compliment you on its flight. Not a bad way to begin a conversation.

Outdoor Festivals

Particularly in warmer weather, many towns and cities organize outdoor concerts, theater productions, art exhibitions, and street fairs. The informality outdoors is conducive to making new acquaintances.

Libraries

I had a college friend, a history major, who wanted to marry a doctor. She did her studying every night in the medical school library. She dated several medical students and eventually married a surgeon.

Most public libraries have very comfortable reading rooms. They're a good place to work or catch up on your magazine reading. Although you'll get shushed for talking above a whisper, you can follow up on your eye contact in the lobby or arrange to meet for coffee. Think about passing a note on the back of a library slip.

You can also meet fellow library users at the computer terminals, or on line waiting for one to be free. If your vision is good, you can check out what the people ahead of you are looking up, and use that information to start a (quiet) discussion.

 ## Cafés

If you find one you like—where the food is appealing, the service friendly, and they let you sit as long as you like—you'll gradually get to know the other regulars and will feel comfortable talking to them as well as newcomers. Make it a place you call home. But don't let that stop you from trying new spots too. Of course if you live in a rural or suburban area, you might not have too many choices as to where you can sip coffee. Try the next town if it's not too far away. Once you've found a place, try sending a drink, with your compliments, to the man glancing at you from across the room.

 ## Bars and Pubs

The "bar scene" can be dating paradise or a nightmare. The key to meeting the kind of men you'd like to meet—if you want to try doing so in a bar—is to frequent a place that's friendly and comfortable, with an atmosphere you enjoy. It might be a good idea to avoid places that are known as singles' bars or pick-up places.

As with cafés, find a place of your own that fits your interests or personality. Bars don't have as much to do with heavy drinking the way they once did, and there's a richness of choice among them. Select a neighborhood pub, a watering hole with a sports or literary bent, or someplace with a great juke box or live country music, or go to happy hour at a university pub. The ambiance of bars, especially those that are neighborhood hangouts, can change according to the time of day. There's an after-five crowd of working people, a later crew of people out for dinner or for the evening, and next a group of people who love the night hours.

Get to know the bartender; he or she might be able to introduce you to other customers.

 ## Bookstores

Booklovers will find many like-minded people who delight in spending time looking at new and old books. Linger in the sections you like best. Feel free to make bookish conversation with anyone you meet in the stacks. If you notice someone flipping through travel guides to Italy, tell him about the not-to-be-missed restaurant you adore in Rome. Or ask the man looking at the jacket of Toni Morrison's newest book if he knows if it's supposed to be as good as her earlier works.

Superstores, which have opened around the country featuring cafés and reading areas along with their extensive offerings, can be a one-stop place for meeting and dating smart men.

Expansive newsstands and stores devoted to magazines are also prime spots for serious browsing and literary talk.

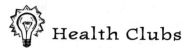 ## Health Clubs

Lots of smart men want to improve their bodies too. The "frequent sightings" principle works here as well. Once you've seen someone often, it will seem natural to initiate a conversation. Keep in mind that people enjoy sharing opinions about the benefits of various types of exercise and like to compare progress. Relax in the co-ed sauna, steam room, or hot tub;

you'll feel great and you'll find a congenial forum for discussion. You can follow up on your initial conversations or introductions when you're dressed.

Certain gyms and health clubs are more social than others; most have their own style. Before you join you are usually allowed a tour or a one-day pass. Be sure you notice who is working out there and how they appear. If you're not comfortable exercising next to others in makeup and carefully matched outfits, find a gym where old sweatshirts are de rigueur.

If a big gym isn't your style, you may try working out at home with a personal trainer. Who knows, while working out you may soon find yourself working on a date.

 BEST ACTIVITIES

 Public Lectures

Find a subject or speaker of interest, and choose your seat wisely. Place yourself near someone who looks interesting, and leave open seats around you for potentially pleasant surprises. Recently, while waiting for a lecture to begin, I watched a woman in front of me signal to a man looking for a seat that there was a free seat next to hers. He followed her suggestion, and when he sat down I realized that she had never seen him before. She then offered him some of the candy she was eating, saying that it was "really too much for one person." I didn't see if they left together, but I give her plenty of credit.

Even if you don't sit next to someone interesting, make time to linger afterward. Once you've attended several lectures in a particular field, you'll begin to recognize others who no doubt share your interest.

You can find out about interesting talks around your area by checking the local newspaper listings and telephone directory services. Many cities have either free or pay-per-minute (900 number) recordings about local events. It's a good idea to place your name on the mailing list of museums, libraries, community centers, and other cultural institutions that offer public programs.

Readings

Bookstores, libraries, universities, and galleries host evenings where a featured author reads from a new work and then answers questions or autographs books. They create an intimate mood between writer and reader, and that can be conducive to terrific encounters. Stay around after the program is finished; it can be a great opportunity to follow up, informally, on any questions that were asked—or unasked.

Religious Services/ Institutions

Find an institution whose religious stance is compatible with your own. Try attending their weekly services and see if you are comfortable with the leader, the atmosphere, and range of activities. You might go to several in your area before you select one you'd like to be affiliated with.

When you arrive, follow the same advice as for lectures on seating, unless your congregation has separate seating for men and women. If you attend with some frequency, you'll get to know the regulars and will also recognize newcomers, whom you can welcome. The institution might have special activities for singles, which are worth checking out, at least once. (You can get schedule information from the bulletins or newsletters.)

If you're so inclined, you might want to join a discussion group, choir, or committee and attend meetings in addition to the weekly prayer services. Or you might offer to coordinate the next series of potluck dinners in members' homes, and you'll get to decide who breaks bread with whom. (How this works: You divide the group into hosts and guests, and then assign several guests to one host's home; it's then up to them to arrange who brings what. It's a simple way to encourage members of a group to get to know one another on a more intimate basis.)

Even if you haven't been in a church, synagogue, or mosque since childhood, and even if you're not particularly religious, you might enjoy being part of a caring community. Perhaps you would prefer one of the many ecumenical institutions. And you might agree with those who believe that matches are divinely inspired. Proximity—and prayers—can't hurt.

▲▲

Heidi: Susie, what are you doing?

Susan: Heidi, men rely on first impressions. Oh, God, he's incredible! Heidi, move!

Heidi: What, Susie?

Susan: Just move! The worst thing you can do is cluster. 'Cause then it looks like you just wanna hang around with your girlfriend. But don't look desperate. Men don't want to dance with desperate women. Oh my God! There's one coming. Will you start moving! Trust me.

—from *The Heidi Chronicles*
by Wendy Wasserstein

▼▼▼

Classes/Continuing Education

Courses can be offered at either colleges or universities, for credit or not. Community centers and local high schools also offer adult education courses. You can take practically anything.

Study a language you've always been interested in. The class is all about making conversation, and you can carry on a conversation outside of class as well. Or take up any subject that interests you.

You can usually attend a continuing education class once with the option of dropping out and getting your money back if the teacher, subject, or classmates don't meet your expectations. Whatever your course of study, you can't go too far wrong. You'll have the opportunity to learn something new, even if the handsome fellow you've been sitting next to is married. Besides, he might have a brother or friend . . .

Think about teaching an adult education course in a subject you have some expertise in. Perhaps one of the students who develops a crush on you will be of interest. You might not want to date any students while you're teaching the course, but there's no reason not to keep in touch and explore possibilities once the term is over. The same is true for teachers you have an interest in outside of class.

You won't get college credit, but you can even find courses on topics like flirting, meeting men, and marrying someone wealthy, and sometimes the class is followed by a social, where the instructor will guide you in doing your homework.

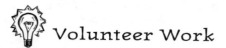 ## Volunteer Work

Being involved with volunteer projects—from work that is very much hands-on, like helping people with special needs, to administrative work that goes beyond stuffing envelopes—is very satisfying in itself. But it's also a great place to come into contact with like-minded people, your fellow volunteers. Their similarly like-minded friends are another important resource for potential dates.

Identify some cause that you're interested in, and then speak to friends or professionals about volunteer opportunities in your community. You can visit home-bound elderly, make recordings for the blind, teach reading to adults or English to new immigrants. I know a woman who married a foreign man she met as his English tutor. Apparently she taught him the right words.

Think about organizing a community project, working on a political campaign, serving on a school committee, wrapping gifts for a holiday toy drive, doing neighborhood advocacy work. You're bound to meet people you'll like if you help run a soup kitchen, give museum tours, advise a youth group, coach a soccer team. A friend dated a man she met as a fellow volunteer at a homeless shelter; they like to joke that they met while spending the night together.

There are a multitude of opportunities to help organizations with fund-raising. In fact, many groups have leadership groups centered on specific age groups, combining social and educational events in order to raise money. Certain people really flourish in organizing events for causes they believe in—and might even have a better time at the planning meetings leading up to the event than at the event itself.

If there's a nonprofit organization whose work you really admire, think about getting more deeply involved, lending your professional skills. Make sure that your interest and involvement are noticed, and perhaps you'll be asked to join the board of directors. Attending board meetings and committee meetings will further your understanding of the group's work and its policies, and will also give you opportunities—and a comfortable atmosphere—to meet fellow board members and staff. No doubt, the work and the people will be interesting. You'll gain in many ways, and contribute to a meaningful cause.

Discussion Groups

If you enjoy sharing opinions on current events, classic texts, the latest best-sellers, or any subject with others, you can join—or start—a weekly or monthly group that meets in members' homes. Some groups are limited to singles; others are not. You can find notices of existing groups (sometimes referred to as "salons") listed in the "personals" sections of newspapers, or check with organizations or community centers to see if they sponsor such groups. Bookstore bulletin boards are a good resource for finding information on book groups that seek new members or individuals interested in creating a group.

 ## Sports

If you like to play tennis, you know that it's not difficult to find male partners. Extend the circle of people you play with; let your (tennis) availability be known. Try playing in tournaments, instructional clinics, or round robins. Become a regular at a club or public court, and if you notice another player you'd like to meet, offer to play with him.

Some sports are best with a group. Offer to crew on someone else's sailboat. Play volleyball, softball, or basketball on co-ed teams. (You're likely to find that men outnumber women at these events.) Join a sports club, and go on ski weekends with a group of friends and their friends. If you like white-water rafting, rock climbing, or sky diving, practice your skill with some fellow adventurers. Run with a buddy, and look for new buddies, or join a runner's club.

If you prefer being a spectator to a participant, get season tickets for your favorite baseball team, and invite a series of guests to go with you. Or you might want to volunteer on the sidelines. A man and woman who met while working—giving out drinks—at the end of a marathon recently got married. There were lots of sneakers at their wedding party.

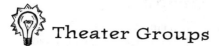 ## Theater Groups

Join a group for those who like attending theater and meet like-minded drama buffs, or if you've always wanted to act, sign up with a community theater troupe. Perhaps you'll play Juliet to an available Romeo. A politician I know once wrote a romantic script for such a group, with leading parts earmarked for himself, of course, and the woman he most wanted to meet. The casting was brilliant, the production not great—but they are now married.

 **Dance**

From Slavic folk dancing to the tango, dance groups hold regularly scheduled sessions, usually including lessons and open dancing. Beginners are welcome. If you're an experienced dancer, you might consider teaching how to do the steps. You'll meet plenty of partners. Try square dancing—you just might like your corners.

▲▲▲▲▲▲▲▲▲▲▲▲▲▲▲▲▲▲▲▲▲▲▲▲▲▲▲▲▲▲▲▲▲▲▲▲▲▲

Last-Minute Escorts (How to Avoid Going Unaccompanied to Your Cousin's Wedding)

1. Anyone's younger brother (as long as he is old enough to vote).
2. Someone you disentangled yourself from—in a kind way— a few months earlier and was friendly the last time you met.
3. The best friend of the man who disentangled himself from you six months earlier.
4. Your best friend's former boyfriend.
5. An unemployed friend who dreams of buffet tables (with a promise that he'll go gently on the hors d'oeuvres).

▼▼▼▼▼▼▼▼▼▼▼▼▼▼▼▼▼▼▼▼▼▼▼▼▼▼▼▼▼▼▼▼▼▼▼▼▼▼

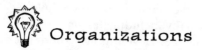 Shopping

I know a woman who dated a man she met in line in a supermarket, and another who met someone at the tie counter in a department store while buying a gift for her brother. Sporting goods stores, bookshops, and music stores can be great for all kinds of browsing. Check out the selections, check out other shoppers, and ask questions.

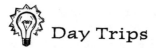 Organizations

Focus on the activities you enjoy most. Join a nature society, an investment club, a political action organization, or an ethnic cultural group. You may enjoy the meetings, activities, or simply receiving the mailings. If you have children, think about specific organizations for single parents.

 Day Trips

Join an organized group for a walking tour of a neighborhood you haven't yet explored, or sign up for a one-day bus trip to a nearby site you've meant to visit. Link up with a group that's going hiking through fall foliage–decorated woods or looking at city architecture. The odds are in your favor that you'll meet some people you'll want to see again.

 Vacations

A period of relaxation brings out the best in many people, so vacations can be ideal meeting grounds. Think of traveling with a tour group (check with travel agents for recommendations; also, museums and community organizations sponsor interesting trips). Go to language school for a week or two. You can study Spanish in Mexico or French in Paris, with lots of adventures between classes. Consider attending a tennis camp or a health spa (ask about the ratio of women to men when you call for information).

If you love traveling and don't have a partner, try going alone. Some people find being on their own in foreign places is more conducive to meeting people than being in a group. Many single travelers report that people go out of their way to show kindness to a single woman. If you haven't done it before, you'll be surprised at how effortless it can be to meet people. Do take some caution. For a first expedition alone, you might want to try being away for a short time.

Consider Club Med. The relaxed atmosphere, beautiful settings, and range of activities make for easy socializing. Friends who were certain that they wouldn't like it—because they weren't "Club Med types"—loved their vacations there and have gone again. Talk to a travel agent you trust about the varying atmospheres at the different locations, and try one that sounds appealing. For a first visit, you might want to seek out a Club that's not specifically for singles; a mixed crowd of singles and couples can be more comfortable. It's an easy trip to do on your own, or coordinate plans with a friend. Single parents might enjoy a Club Med vacation with their kids at one of the family resorts. Great times await you.

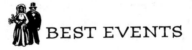 ## BEST EVENTS

 ## Weddings

The air is fragrant with romance and possibility, and the dressed-up guests are looking their best. Magical connections are frequently made at weddings. Enjoy; try not to be blue that you're not the one in white. At least you're not stuck wearing a bridesmaid's dress (and if you are, take solace in the fact that you never have to wear it again. Maybe you can use it as a conversation starter.) Weddings are comfortable places to introduce yourself to anyone you don't know—you can always ask how they know the bride and/or groom. At those celebrations that are weekend affairs, you'll have many opportunities to round up potential dates. If all else fails, you can remember what you like and don't like about the festivities—it will be essential information when you plan your own.

High School Reunions

If at all possible, go back to your hometown for these events. You might be pleasantly surprised by who else shows up—and it's astonishing what twenty-five, ten, even five years out of school, perhaps out of town, can do for that brainy, quiet kid you dissected a frog with in eleventh-grade biology. Reconnecting with old pals—as well as those you were either too cool or too shy to talk with then—can make for great new alliances.

College Reunions

There are usually fewer surprises here than at high school reunions, but no fewer possibilities to reconnect and rekindle a romance or friendship. Even if you boycotted graduation and can't remember the words to the school song, try going to your class reunion.

College Alumni Events

Chances are pretty good that you'll find someone with similar interests at a reception given by your college or university.

There's always the possibility of renewing relationships of another era. Conversation flows at these events and even if you know everyone in your graduating class, you may not *yet* know great men who were in classes just ahead of you or behind you.

There's a popular saying at Middlebury College in Vermont that more of its alumni marry each other than do graduates of any other college; in fact, it's said that two out of three students marry another graduate. There's no statistical evidence to back this up, and it might be more folklore than fact. A former chaplain at the school who has officiated at many alumni weddings told a *New York Times* reporter that Middlebury graduates tend to stay in touch after graduation and attend annual alumni events, which he believes lead to marriages.

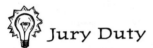 Jury Duty

Look on the bright side when you get your next summons to participate on a jury. You'll meet lots of potentially interesting people you wouldn't know otherwise. As you're listening to all the facts, be aware of everyone else involved in the courtroom drama. You'll have plenty to talk about while you wait around the jury room or during lunch break. You might even get sequestered with some of them.

And if you don't get selected for a jury and spend your days waiting, as is the case in some cities, you'll get to know many fellow jurors by name by hearing roll call again and again. You may quickly feel like you're among friends. After a recent stint on a jury, I introduced one fellow juror to a friend looking for a new secretary, and another to a friend for a date. Justice for all.

On Arriving, Exiting, and Waiting

This isn't existential but rather practical advice. You can meet interesting people as you're entering a museum or leaving a movie. Conversations are almost inevitable.

Waiting time is really ripe for talk too. When you're waiting at the sports center for your squash court, sitting in your ophthalmologist's office, or waiting your turn to pick up your order at the deli, you're likely to be surrounded by people who are similarly engaged, all committed to that particular place for at least a while. Yes, you're stuck there but it's also an opportunity. Your fellow waiters (not the servers) might be daydreaming, reading, wondering about you, or fretting about the time. Many would welcome friendly conversation. Go for it.

When possible, design your waiting time. If you're planning to meet a friend, select a place that's congenial to wait in. Cafés, public atriums, and hotel lobbies are good places to rest and look around.

Think of the intervals when you wait as pleasant pauses. You might make a habit of arriving early.

Try several of these suggestions, and keep trying until you find what's most comfortable for you. If you prefer not to experience these adventures solo, invite a friend to go along. Some women enjoy the dynamics of going out with two friends, finding that a threesome gives each the benefits of freedom and support when needed.

Be sure to choose companions who won't cling to you like lycra, are upbeat, and bring out your splendid spirit. Introduce each other to everyone you know when you arrive. It's a good idea to devise a plan beforehand—a secret code or sign language that can be flashed across a room—so that you alert one another if you'd prefer to leave with someone else or if you want them to remain on guard at your side.

Many women prefer to go out alone. Being on your own can mean being more approachable. Do what's most comfortable for you, but if you choose the solo route, use some ordinary caution. Yes, it's great to be open to the men you encounter, but don't forget altogether what your parents told you about talking to strangers.

More Great Places to Meet Great Men

They gave each other a smile with a future in it.
—Ring Lardner

Personally I can't see why it would be any less romantic to find a husband in a nice four-color catalogue than in the average downtown bar at happy hour.

—Barbara Ehrenreich

$\mathcal{E}$ven if you follow every piece of advice in the last chapter, you won't have exhausted the possibilities. On a daily basis, additional men are moving to your city and others are becoming available for any number of reasons. Still others are showing signs of genuine interest in dating. The newly arrived, newly available, and newly ready are prime candidates. You've got to help them find you.

Beyond going places and joining groups related to your interests, you can take action, at home and at work too. You can also avail yourself of the many services designed specifically to aid people in meeting significant others. Don't be turned off if some activity has *single* in the title. Your vision that the participants would be a pathetic bunch whose mothers had signed them up or, even worse, a reunion of all your worst blind dates is just not true. Many who participate are just like you—intelligent, attractive people who are open to meeting new people, and are experimenting with all sorts of avenues to do so.

Think of yourself as a pioneer or an explorer in new territory. Here are additional proven-successful strategies.

 At Home

Have a party. Invite ten unattached women friends and ask each to bring two or three great single men. In your invitation, be clear to each friend that her guests can be friends, old boyfriends, brothers, or any males she thinks others might enjoy meeting—the type she might even date herself. Keep the mood informal; the idea works best as a Sunday brunch, cocktail party during the week, or casual weekend evening get-together. Think of it as a recycling event, or a fabulous sale in a secondhand shop. It's highly likely that one person will be thrilled with another's rejects. Since some men inevitably won't show at the last minute, you might even think of a 1:4 ratio. You don't have to tell the men the exact nature of the party.

At Work

Office romance can be problematic, but not impossible, depending on the atmosphere of your workplace. Be careful. Dating your boss can be dangerous and isn't always recommended, but you might think about people you meet through your work. Consider people who work in other departments or whom you work with only on an occasional basis. Some possible nonbusiness liaisons include (the timing is critical) lawyers and clients (after a case is completed), publicists and producers, editors and writers (once the book is finished), actors and directors, reporters and subjects (once the story is published), museum curators and designers, bankers and brokers (after the deal is done). It can be a good idea to keep things platonic while you are actually working together and then follow up with a date invitation after the work is completed.

Do keep in touch with coworkers you admire who change jobs, or your former colleagues when you make a career move. It might be more comfortable to become romantically involved with someone you've worked closely with, perhaps traveled with, once your paychecks come from different sources.

Don't rule out people in your field whose work competes with your own. No doubt you share interests with men involved in similar efforts, even if they represent the other side. Remember the romance of James Carville and Mary Matalin? They married after dating through the 1992 presidential elections, when they designed campaign tactics for opposing candidates.

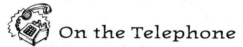 ## On the Telephone

Yes, I know someone who dated a wrong number. He called her looking for someone else; she liked the sound of his voice and stayed on the line. They met a day later for lunch, and they've been married for twenty-five years. It was indeed the right number. The lesson: Don't hang up so quickly on someone who has misdialed.

If you enjoy talking on the telephone, it's likely that you have phone friendships with people you've never met, whether through work or other activities. Try getting together in person with one of the (single) men who's been on the line. A friend who works in sales and makes lots of fast friends on the phone has a great time at such meetings. It's easier, she says, than an ordinary blind date because she feels like she already knows the man.

You'll be surprised at how physical appearances match up to voices and manners. Whether dazzling or disappointing, it's always interesting.

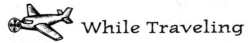 While Traveling

Choose a seat carefully when you set out by bus or train. On longer trips, be particularly careful. Inter-city trains might be your best opportunity. You can take control by selecting a seat next to a person who looks like someone you'd like to get to know instead of sitting alone and waiting for someone to join you. Wander through the cars until you see a place you like, and take it—you can easily move if you discover you're not interested in pursuing a conversation. Or just enjoy the panoramic view from your window. It's a good idea to keep a book or magazine handy if you find you'd rather not talk.

When you're flying, you have less of a say in who your seatmates will be, as seats are assigned before you board. Airport lounges—especially since flights are so frequently delayed—can be conducive to conversation with your fellow travelers. If you want to continue a conversation during the flight, you might be able to change your seat. You can try asking the person assigned to the seat next to you—or next to the gentleman you'd like to sit with—whether he or she would mind switching seats so that you can sit with the person you're traveling with. Or, when you board, you might be pleasantly surprised by who's located across the aisle.

You don't have to travel far to encounter interesting new people. Look at more than the advertisements when you're on buses, trolleys, and subways. Don't hesitate to make eye contact, smile, or initiate a conversation. In a setting when people don't expect conviviality, a friendly gesture can be most welcome. (A basic reminder: If you meet someone literally "on the street" or in some other casual setting, it's best to spend any additional time in a public place, whether having a drink or coffee or going for a walk. Think twice, and then again, before inviting a stranger to your home. If you're unsure about someone, give them your work—rather than home—telephone number.)

Here's another travel idea. When you go to a different city, whether for work or a social visit, spend some time with that city's phone book. Look up old friends you've lost contact with; think about men or women you know from high school, summer camp, graduate school, or that you met on vacation. You might enjoy the renewed connections, and perhaps you will finally go out on a date with your costar from summer-stock productions. Also, your friends might make some interesting dating connections for you during your stay.

Romance Brokers

The services of a professional matchmaker—some call themselves human relations specialists—can cost plenty of money, and there are no guarantees. I'm convinced that you'll do as well by using the free matchmaking services of friends and relatives, once you have them trained (see Chapter 3). But if you're curious as to what a "romance broker" can do, check the yellow pages or local newspapers for listings under "marriage brokers" or "matrimonial services," and make an information-only appointment. Some matchmakers have connections with colleagues in their vicinity as well as in other cities, and frequently pool resources. Many claim to have impressive track records. Since some matchmakers do all of their prospecting within a particular ethnic group, you might be well served by them if it's important that you meet someone from your religious or ethnic community.

Dating services, many of which are run by professionals with advanced degrees in fields like social work and psychology, work in a similar way. They usually promise to arrange a certain number of dates, and rely on detailed questionnaires and personal interviews to make their recommendations. Some allow participants to view the applications of others in order to screen and select potential dates.

Lunch-dating Services

Many cities have agencies that specialize in arranging matches over lunch in the downtown area for working people. A great way for busy people to fit in blind dates, these services have been described as business lunches where the business is romance. The agencies charge clients a fee for arranging a set number of lunch dates; they usually take charge of selecting the restaurant and making reservations. At the end of the meal, the bill is split (Dutch treat) and business cards are exchanged—or not.

Singles-only Events

Many organizations devoted to single people arrange tennis parties, ski trips, holiday dances, and more, usually geared to specific age groups like twentysomething or thirty-five to fifty. Most of the events are advertised in local newspapers, and once you're added to a group's mailing list, you're on it for life. Some women find the atmosphere of events exclusively for singles to be too pressured, and prefer to attend social gatherings in more natural settings, where a variety of people are present.

If you cringe when you hear the words *singles only* and imagine "getting to know you" events that are a cross between junior high school socials and group therapy, you may want to reconsider your point of view. Not all group meetings will make you wish you stayed home. Singles groups do vary, based on their membership and the organizers' style. Some have a down-to-earth spirit and others are more formal; you'll find intimate gatherings as well as events that promise record-breaking attendance. The promotional literature of one organization quotes a member who describes the group as her extended family. (Let's hope she has many brothers.)

Singles programs might afford you opportunities to participate in interesting activities you wouldn't otherwise. In recent years, groups dedicated to hiking, outdoors adventures, theater, museums, social and political issues, and other interests have been formed.

Singles-only gourmet dining clubs, now operating in many cities, offer evenings at well regarded restaurants, beginning with a cocktail hour and then a sit-down brunch or dinner. Some groups charge membership fees (in addition to the individual dinner costs); others require payment only for those dinners attended. The degree of spontaneity varies, with certain organizers planning every detail, including specific seating arrangements and the menu. Some groups also offer combined dinner and theater events. For people who enjoy dining out, these groups provide congenial settings to meet new people and try a wide range of restaurants. Reciprocal memberships in other cities may be available, so that if you are traveling, you can hook up with a local group for meals.

If a particular singles activity is of interest, try it; you can take comfort in the fact that you don't have to stay until the end if it's not to your liking. A word of caution: Beware of singles-only boat rides. You might not be able to disembark at the moment when you've had more than enough mingling. However, keep in mind that I know a married couple who met on an all-singles ferry ride around Manhattan.

Singles Newsletters

Groups with special interests like science, new age, or classical music have recently launched networks that enable like-minded people to connect. Also known as exchanges, additional groups bring together individuals with academic backgrounds and interest in the arts; there's also a group that specializes in links between younger women and older men as well as older women and younger men. The promoters of these groups boast of many marriages as well as lasting friendships that have developed among members.

Each group operates differently, but most follow a system something like this: After you join, you submit a biographical profile in two formats, short and long. The short versions (like personal ads) of every member are printed in the group's monthly newsletter. Once you receive the newsletter, you can request to see the longer biographies, which include addresses and phone numbers, of those people who sound appealing. Then you can call or write them and arrange to meet. Members are entitled to receive a certain number of bios for free and pay a fee for additional copies. Some networks simply forward your letters after you see the newsletter. The financial costs of participating are quite modest.

In some ways, this is a more focused version of placing a personal ad, and it's also more equitable. You'll be making the calls as well as receiving them. And when someone contacts you, you might already have his bio in your file. However, since many networks are not specific to a particular region, a botanist in Florida might strike up a relationship with a geologist in Colorado. But don't forget there are rocks to be found in Florida, and plants in Colorado. The point is to meet people and make new connections.

You can obtain information about the various groups by responding to the small classified ads they place in both general-interest and specialized magazines. Check the listings under

"Singles." I first learned about a "conscious singles"/new age network through a vegetarian foods magazine and about an academic group through a literary journal.

Personal Ads

They work; in fact, it's commonplace to hear of happily married couples who met through the personals, as personal classified advertisements are known. But it takes some work—devising an ad, writing letters, and responding—to try out the system.

There are pros and cons to being the advertiser (placing the ad yourself) or the respondent. You might try doing both at the same time, and see how you're most comfortable. (I was always reticent to respond to an ad out of fear that, since I had dated so much, I would already know the man whose ad I was answering.)

Either way, it's a waiting game. Responding to an ad means waiting for the "handsome nonsmoking dad" or the "physician seeking soulmate" to call you back. Sometimes men get so many responses that even if your notes or messages are brilliant, it might take some time for them to get in touch. If you do answer an ad, keep a copy of it along with a copy of your response. That way, when he calls you'll have a clear idea of his identity. Especially if you answer several ads at the same time—which is a good idea—it's easy to confuse the incoming callers. (Try not to ask, "Which one are you?")

When you run an ad, you'll have to wait for the respondents to answer. But you take control by sifting through the pile and calling them back—or not. Placing an ad does entail some expense on your part as well as investing the time in writing an effective ad.

Many newspapers and magazines that feature personal ads now offer voice-mail systems in which you can leave telephone messages as responses to specific ads, in the same way you would leave a message on someone's home answering machine. In some systems, it's the person behind the ad who actually records the message, so callers have the opportunity to listen to the voice for any telling clues before responding. With voice mail, responding to an ad is almost effortless. But be aware of the costs of using toll (900) telephone numbers.

When You Answer an Ad

Browse through the listings in several newspapers, magazines, and journals you like, and select a few ads that sound appealing. You'll need to check the particular code system employed to make sense of such abbreviations as NS, NR, DWM, and NM. Also, each publication has slightly different rules for responding, so be sure to follow the specific instructions listed. Each publication, as you'll learn, attracts a different type of advertiser as well as respondent.

Your response, whether by phone or note, should be brief. Tell enough to catch the ad writer's attention so that he'll want to call you back. You may want to provide your work number, if that's appropriate. You don't have to provide a biography or a checklist of how you match up to the qualities listed in his ad. Keep it simple, perhaps a bit mysterious; don't give him any information—for instance, you just lost your job, this will be your first date after a complicated divorce—that will land your letter in the "if all else fails" pile. In your response, you might refer to one item mentioned in the ad, and then in a friendly, upbeat way say that you'd be interested in figuring out a time when you can get together.

(The process is not unlike applying for a job. In that situation, you know that your cover letter should say enough about you so that the employer will be curious to interview you. You don't need to include information like salary history, whether you'd relocate—even if they ask for it. You don't want to give them reasons to eliminate you on the basis of your answers. The goal is to get an interview. Then you'll have the opportunity in person to persuade them of your fine qualities, no matter what their prior expectations.)

▲▲

(Scene in a restaurant)

Prudence: Hello.

Bruce: Hello.

Prudence: Are you the white male, thirty to thirty-five, six-foot-two, blue eyes, who's into rock music, movies, jogging and quiet evenings at home?

Bruce: Yes, I am.

Prudence: Hi, I'm Prudence.

Bruce: I'm Bruce.

Prudence: Nice to meet you.

Bruce: Won't you sit down?

Prudence: Thank you. As I said in my letter, I've never answered one of these ads before.

Bruce: Me neither. I mean, I haven't put one in before.

Prudence: But this time I figured, why not?

Bruce: Right. Me too. I hope I'm not too macho for you.

Prudence: No. So far you seem wonderful.

Bruce: You have lovely breasts. That's the first thing I notice in a woman.

Prudence: Thank you.

Bruce: You have beautiful contact lenses.

Prudence: I like the timbre of your voice. Soft but firm.

Bruce: Thanks. I like *your* voice.

Prudence: Thank you. I love the smell of Brut you're wearing.

Bruce: Thank you. My male lover Bob gave it to me.

—from *Beyond Therapy* by
Christopher Durang

▼▼

Another way to get someone's attention is to send an unusual postcard or clever greeting card with a short note. It's also fine to use any stationery you like or a plain sheet of white paper. If your handwriting looks childish or is near illegible, type your response. If you use a personal computer it will be simple to keep records—but be sure that your response doesn't read like a form letter.

You might want to include only your phone number and not your address. There are too many stories of dangerous characters lurking behind sweet-sounding ads. Your safety and comfort are of the utmost importance. Along those lines, you'll want to be sure to have your first meeting with someone you meet through the personals in a public, well-trafficked place rather than your home or his (see p. 99).

The same advice applies to voice mail, when the service is available. Keep your responses brief, cheerful, and confident.

Photographs

Some advertisers request photos, others don't. It's your call whether to send one. It's a simple fact that appearance plays a role here. If you have a photo you like, include it. However, if you think no photo does you justice, or if you don't like the idea of someone looking you over before deciding whether to call, don't send one. If a man uses that as a reason not to call, he may not have been someone for you in any case. But if you find that you're getting scant response to your witty pictureless letters, you might reconsider. Have a friend shoot a roll of film of you in an informal setting, and you're bound to have some good results. One friend who chooses not to include a photo ends her letters with a postscript: "I'm not enclosing a photo, but you won't be disappointed." She gets called back.

When You Place an Ad

Look at the personals in several monthly, weekly, and daily publications you either read regularly or would read if you had time. To begin, select the one or two places to run your ad based on (1) whether you can imagine someone you'd want to meet reading it, and (2) whether you're comfortable with the format of the personals section. You'll reach a different audience using a literary weekly like *The New York Review of Books* than a city magazine like *Los Angeles* or *Philadelphia*, or an ethnic-interest or sports weekly, so you'll want to place your ad according to your priorities. Check if any of the weekly newspapers in your city offer free personal ads—that might be a good place to experiment.

If you select a publication whose audience is local rather than national, you're more likely to hear from people who live nearby, which will make getting together in person possible. If you don't mind corresponding by mail and telephone before one of you ventures to visit the other's city, consider a national magazine that reflects your interests. Think about college and graduate school alumni publications as well as community and special-interest newspapers. A Russophile I know placed an ad in a Russian-language newspaper, and now has a Russian spouse.

Frequency

Arrange for the ad to appear more than once, because someone who *should* see it might miss the first issue. Depending on the cost and how much money you want to spend, run the ad a few times in different places. You might begin, though, with one publication, to test how the whole system works and whether you're comfortable with it.

Wording the Ad

Spend some time reading the personals to get an idea of the range of styles. You'll notice that most ads have two components: a headline, in bold type, and a few sentences of snappy copy. Unless you make your living creating award-winning headlines, you should avoid the impulse to devise a line that will stand out—and try something straightforward. Interesting juxtapositions work well, and alliteration (BRIGHT BRITISH BROKER) gets attention most of the time. Sometimes headlines that try to be too clever fall short of that—and fall flat.

▲▲▲

Sample Ad Headlines (clipped from newspapers and magazines)

In:

I'M IN THE MOOD FOR LOVE*

212/MD

GRACIOUS, SPUNKY, PENSIVE

WISE GUY WANTED

BLONDE PREFERS GENTLEMAN

Out:

MS. RIGHT AVAILABLE

NATALIE WOOD LOOKALIKE**

A IS FOR ADORABLE, B IS FOR BRUNETTE

PRETTY BRIGHT WOMAN***

CLASS ACT SEEKS HER MATCH

STOP HERE! COMPLETE PACKAGE

* The woman who used this received more than fifty responses.
** Don't say it unless it's absolutely true.
*** Apparently, the intended comma between *pretty* and *bright* was lost in production. Be careful of how your line reads if punctuation is omitted.

▼▼▼

Since Nora Ephron's film *Sleepless in Seattle* was released, headlines like SLEEPLESS IN SUBURBIA have been popular. You'll find lots of variations on David Letterman's "Top Ten" lists, and many ads that boast that this is the person's first ad ever. There's no right way to write an ad; different people will obviously find different approaches appealing.

In the text of the ad, do try to say something that's distinctive about you. It's best to invent a phrase that doesn't appear in every other ad you see (who doesn't enjoy candlelight dinners?). It's also fine to model your ad closely on another one that strikes you. Include age, race, religion, and profession if those are important to you. Avoid the word *unique*, and play with the sequence of words and abbreviations until you come up with something you like, but don't fuss too much. Simple is just fine.

If you're having trouble getting started, ask a friend for suggestions. Don't worry about creating a perfect ad; go with the best choice you have. You can always amend it.

Many advertising clerks and managers who work on the personals sections of publications—whom you'll speak to if you call in your ad—are quite seasoned at what they do and might offer helpful and valid suggestions on the ad's content.

 Waiting

Don't worry if the responses are slow in arriving. For the same reason that it took you two weeks to write the ad, it might take someone several weeks to compose a response and mail it. Some people hold ads for weeks before answering them. Also, if the responses are sent to a box number at the publication, it might take some days, even weeks, before the letters are forwarded to you.

Responding to Responses

When you have the letters in hand, call as many as you can. I'd say call them all, unless you get hundreds of responses, or someone sounds clearly objectionable, or if you're five-foot-nine and he's five-foot-one and you're absolutely sure that would be a turnoff—but don't be too sure. Try not to eliminate anyone on the basis of poor penmanship or dull phrasing; some men, and women too, are more charming in person than on paper.

Rank the responses according to your interest level and call the first few on top of the pile. You might chat briefly but try to bring the conversation to a quick closure, arranging a time to get together. You don't want to be interviewed or to conduct an interview by telephone. Save that conversation for your first meeting. Again, try not to judge someone on the basis of their phone manner. For some wonderful people, it's just not a strength. If they've gone to the trouble of responding, and you've made the effort to call them, it's worth your while to take another step and get together. You don't have to commit to anything more than a cup of coffee. (See Chapter 9 for suggestions on arranging a great first meeting.)

Once you have gone through the first group of responses and decide that you've found someone nice but want to see who else is out there, or determined that all the ones you've met are already married; better as friends; creeps/jerks/bores; too old/young, fat/skinny, religious/not religious, loud/quiet; or more appropriate for your best friend, start calling the next batch.

Taking Stock

Professional marketers frequently reevaluate and reposition their advertising plans based on reactions. If you're not satisfied with either the quality or quantity of responses, think about trying different publications. You might also want to try out a variation on the ad itself, or consider a larger size, perhaps with a decorative border, that will really stand out.

Some publications allow you to place personal ads in other sections where they really stand out. A woman whose ad ran in the "sports car" section got a great response. Too bad that, as of yet, *The Wall Street Journal* and *Esquire* don't take personal ads.

 ## Group Ads

A variation on personal ads, these are small ads placed by a circle of friends seeking to get together with a group of men for a particular event, like a dinner, bridge tournament, or canoe trip. There's a certain comfort in meeting strangers within the company of friends. Once you get the agreed-on number of respondents to your ad, which should be about equal to the number of women participating, set a place and time and alert your friends and potential new friends. The "group date" can be great fun, as well as a tool for extending your contacts, but be prepared for the inevitability that several friends may find the same male guest intriguing.

Computer Networks

Thanks to modern telecommunications technology, you have the potential to connect with like-minded people nationwide in a nonpressured style, without leaving your home. All you need is a personal computer, a modem, some appropriate software—and a little bit of high-tech know-how (or a friend with such).

Several large-scale and well-known computer services companies, as well as some boutique operations, offer subscribers access to various bulletin boards and on-line services. They provide instructions that even computer novices can make sense of. Individuals can post messages on a variety of topics from rock music to linguistics to financial advice, and invite personal response. Communication via notes and letters might be anonymous or signed, instantaneous or delayed, public or private, depending on the particular service. Subscribers can "eavesdrop" on others' conversations before joining in. If you decide you don't like the company, you can simply log off—a painless, almost effortless good-night.

A woman who spends hours a day logged onto her network speaks of the computer as a great "equalizer" in meeting new people: Physical attractiveness takes a backseat to honest, witty communication. With computer communications, body language is expressed through abbreviations, punctuation, and capitalization, and the systems have their particular "netiquette."

For those who insist on having their first conversations with men over espresso, there are coffeehouses in northern California that feature tabletop computer terminals. Customers can log on and converse with new acquaintances while enjoying the café's ambiance. There are plans to expand the idea nationwide.

Recent newspaper and magazine stories (LOVE AT FIRST BYTE is the classic headline) have chronicled the stories of couples who met and married after meeting through computer networks. One couple held their marriage service "on line" with people around the country participating. I particularly like a story of a woman who posted a poem she wrote, and later married a man who was moved by it.

 ## Video Dating

If you're telegenic, you might enjoy signing up with a service that, for a set fee, allows you to make a personal videotape, usually a short statement about your interests and what you're looking for in a mate—like a personal ad with the added bonus of a visual picture. You get to preview your dates, and they get an advance view of you too. Your tape will be viewed by men who sign up and you can view theirs; if there's mutual interest in the tapes, the service will arrange for you to meet in person.

Before making the tape, think about your "pitch"—what you want to say about yourself. You might want to have a friend shoot a rehearsal tape with a home video camera so that you can amend your statement before you record with the service. Remember that you'll be filmed from the waist up. Avoid wearing bright white or red; light blue is fine and so are navy, burgundy, green, and purple; don't wear horizontal stripes (look at what television anchors wear on camera and you'll get a good sense of what works best). It's best not to look directly into the camera, but at a spot nearby, and don't stare. Smile.

Television Game Shows

With names like *Love Connection*, *Love at First Sight*, and *Studs*, television shows are playing matchmaker on the air. Contestants appear on these shows with the hopes of finding a perfect mate (and perhaps furthering their theatrical careers). The lingo is sexual innuendo. These new shows make *The Dating Game*, an earlier version of media mating that aired twenty-five years ago, look like a church social with parental chaperones.

I know of one joyously married couple with two children who made their "love connection" on national television. If the idea appeals to you, think about becoming a contestant. Before you sign up, I recommend that you watch one of these shows—once—and you'll realize that you're already on a much better track to meeting an intelligent man.

 The Next Wave

As technology continues to evolve, so too do new opportunities for making bonds with interesting men. Interactive television projects are being developed, so it might not be too long before there are possibilities of meeting people from the comfort of your sofa using your remote control. Virtual reality technology might bring the experience of blind dating to a new realm altogether.

More Smart Strategies

▶ Walk your dog to a place where other animal owners congregate. Your pet might lead you in a promising direction. If you don't have a dog, borrow one. (It's an old trick of the trade; private detectives use dogs for this reason: People seem to talk easily to others with dogs.) Similarly, feel free to make conversation with a man you see out walking his dog—many male dog walkers are using this strategy to meet you.

▶ Volunteer to attend work-related conferences and meetings out of town. Along with potential interesting men you'll meet during the proceedings, you'll have opportunities while traveling and in your free time (follow advice the on page 61 on traveling).

▶ Skip the convenience of doing your laundry in your home and bring your soiled stuff to a public laundromat. Some businesses have cafés, video rooms, and even exercise equipment where patrons can spend their waiting time instead of watching their clothing tumble dry. Even in an old-fashioned laundromat, your curiosity about the nicely tailored shirts washing next to yours might lead you to meet their owner.

▶ If you're a single parent—or would like to meet someone with kids—the obvious places like park playgrounds and kids' activities provide optimum opportunities for meeting single parents. Little League practice is a super place to strike up a conversation.

▶ Usher at a local theater. The many benefits include seeing a show for free, meeting the other ushers and perhaps the cast, and greeting the theatergoers, one of whom you might want to greet again when the show is over.

▶ Get a pair of season tickets to the ballet or theater company. Invite someone different—an old friend or an acquaintance you'd like to know better—to join you for each performance. He may not be the one for you, but he might have friends.

▶ Attend a wine-tasting at a local vineyard, restaurant, or cooking school. You'll be clicking glasses in no time.

▶ Organize a reunion of your yoga class, old friends from camp, former colleagues, college acting troupe, neighbors past and present, and so on. Make sure the date is convenient for the man you're most curious about seeing again.

▶ You'll never know if the driver of your taxi is an underemployed Ph.D. or an artist, actor, or novelist about to make it big unless you relax and engage him in conversation. Make the best use of your riding time. If you have no interest in the conversation as it proceeds, pay your fare and you're likely to never see the man again.

▶ Call to order a copy of *Alaska Men* magazine (907-522-1492) or *Bachelor Book* (305-341-8801) and look over their offerings of mail-order dates. Some of the men featured seem down to earth and charming. You never know.

▶ Rent a bicycle built for two and ride around a local park. You'll be noticed—and you can offer the back seat to anyone who looks interesting. I saw a man do this, with admirable grace and seeming success; I think a woman rider would fare well, too.

▶ Write a great letter. If there's someone you know of, and you can't think of anyone you know who might know him, send him a note telling him that you'd like to meet him. Try writing to someone profiled in the newspaper, or to a writer, artist, public official, or activist whose work you admire. He's likely to be charmed, intrigued, and inspired to invite you to dinner.

▶ Wear a fabulous hat. You'll no doubt receive comments, and you may want to respond—selectively.

▶ Give a dinner party. Ask your neighbor to invite the friend you noticed at his door.

▶ Rent a booth at a local fair and sell your handicrafts. Or have some fun with a friend and sell advice—to raise money for a cause you care about.

▶ Take a share in a summer house with a group of men and women. It's best if you know only a few of them, or even no one, beforehand.

▶ While I don't recommend getting sick, I love the story of a friend who met her husband the doctor when taken to the emergency room of a hospital.

▶ If you're so inclined, try intense prayer. Some believe in visiting religious sites, receiving special blessings, and/or carrying amulets. A religious leader can be helpful on the specifics.

▶ There's an old Syrian folktale, "One Tooth and Two Tooth," about two spinster sisters in which one, named Two Tooth, schemes to win the hand of the prince for her sister. As he passes below their window, she pours rose water mixed with essence of jasmine and blossoms onto his head, and then instructs her sister One Tooth to exclaim, out of sight, that she accidentally spilled her used bathwater out the window. The prince exclaims that he's smitten with a woman whose bathwater could be so fragrant. The strategy works, and with some subsequent magic, the prince marries One Tooth. They live happily ever after.

▶ Ask couples how they met. You might find wonderful inspiration.

First Words
Flirting With Dignity

Speak low if you speak love.
> —Don Pedro, in Shakespeare's
> *Much Ado About Nothing*

The eyes have one language everywhere.
> —Roumanian proverb

As you are navigating through the many places in which you encounter interesting men, you may be wondering how to get from lectures or ski trips to dates. The step in between is talk.

Initiating Conversation

It hardly matters what your first words are. Say something, anything. Don't worry about sounding wise or sophisticated—

at this stage all he'll notice is that you're being friendly. It's likely that he'll respond in the same vein. Why do you think so many people talk about the weather—because they're truly interested or because it's easy? Break the ice. Say hello. Comment on something you read in the newspaper. You can always offer a compliment. Or ask a question. Do you know if . . . ? Where's the best . . . ? How can I get to . . . ? That gives the other person an opportunity to respond.

When you're traveling in foreign countries, you have an easy first question, whether in your language or his: Do you speak English? In an American town or city, asking a man whether he speaks French isn't a bad conversation opener.

Find common ground. You might be standing on it. If you and a man are in the same place—any place, whether a class, cultural event, department store, or on a bus—there's already a measure of mutuality to build on. If you meet at a reading or concert, your shared presence signals a shared interest and can easily ignite a conversation. The same is only slightly less true if you'd like to meet the person next to you on a train or behind you on line.

You can invite conversation by indicating that you'd welcome it. Being open is being receptive; it doesn't necessarily mean being aggressive. You can be reserved or loud-mouthed—however you're comfortable—and still signal your openness to possibilities. Put away your book on the train; look around while you're waiting on line. (It's great to carry a book or magazine; you make it easy for someone to approach you and ask what you're reading. Try carrying this book face-out, and you're bound to stir up interest.)

There's a reason Victorian women often dropped their handkerchiefs: to attract attention and make contact with a desirable man. You may not carry handkerchiefs, but there are other ways to initiate a conversation. The goal, however you do it, is to look into someone's eyes, to establish a connection. To do so, you have to pay attention to who is around you and be aware of who has their eyes on you. Sometimes eyes have their own dialogues, and following up with words is simple; other times you have to start from scratch.

Remember that silence isn't necessarily failure; it's sometimes part of the process. And sometimes it's quite a relief. Don't panic at conversation lulls. If you can, relax.

You'll know when you encounter someone who just isn't interested in talking to you or to anyone, and when it's not worth trying to draw him out. Don't worry, he's in the minority. Most people will be grateful.

Flirting With Dignity

A friend who pushes herself to go to a lot of cocktail parties tells me that she overcomes her initial shyness at these events by first talking to the waiters and bartenders. It's a warm-up, she says, to gaining courage to approach others she'd like to meet. Before the evening is over, she's worked the room like a pro. (And she once dated a poet/waiter she met at such a gathering.)

Another friend enjoys frequenting cafés and small restaurants by herself. Relaxing over a cup of tea and a book, she manages to survey her surroundings, and makes eye contact with any men who seem interesting. Her charm radiates. It's not unusual for men to pause at her table and chat or ask if they can join her.

I've seen both women in action, and I'd describe their different styles as examples of flirting with dignity. Each one enjoys herself, never lets her self-esteem sink, doesn't compromise herself, and inevitably gives out her phone number a few times—whether for potential dates, joint business ventures, tennis matches, or matchmaking for her friends.

Flirting with dignity is not about being coy or silly. You're too smart for that. It is about communicating openness and self-confidence. Be 100 percent present. Make eye contact—catch an eye, exchange a glance, look for an extra second or two, and flash a real smile. Be friendly, ready to laugh. When conversation begins, be sure to hold up your end, and do more than that: Ask questions, offer comments, make jokes, solicit opinions, guide the dialogue in an interesting direction.

Some women seem to be born with magnetism. But there's no shortage of ways to be appealing. Charm can be ironic, subtle, earthy, even cynical; we're not all bubbly cheerleaders, nor would we want to be. And not every man is drawn to the same type of charm.

If it's difficult to form a mental picture of just how you might send a message that you're open, think of the opposite situation. You know how it feels when you're not interested in someone: you turn your body away, you look down and step back, you are distracted and inattentive, you don't fill the silence. Now reverse those signals, and you're ready to begin.

▲▲▲
Smarts From the Fourth Grade
1. If you like a boy, ask your friend to tell him.
2. Send valentines to all the boys in the class and sign them "from." For the boy you like, write "love."
3. Change seats with the girl who sits next to him.
4. Don't tell your younger sister.
5. Ride your bicycle past his house.
6. Share your dessert at lunch.
7. Chase him during recess.
8. Bump into him during fire drills.
▼▼▼

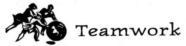 ## Teamwork

Strategize with a single friend, whether male or female. If you're together and one of you starts a conversation with someone, the other can help keep the conversation going and also help to draw the new man into the conversation. In fact, some people feel pressured by one-on-one conversations with someone of the opposite sex, and this format might feel more comfortable for everyone. Once the chatting is going smoothly, you (or your friend—whoever is the "designated third party" in that situation) can slip away and let things proceed on their own.

Your friend can also help rescue you from a situation you can't get away from quickly enough by yourself. Once you and your friend understand each other's subtle signals, you'll not only support each other but can advance each other's efforts in meeting new people.

How to Turn a Brief Exchange into a Date (or at Least a Cup of Coffee)

It's really easier than you might think. When you start talking with someone you meet visiting an art gallery, browsing in a bookstore, or sitting next to you in a class, simply ask, "Would you like to get a cup of coffee?" Even if you feel that's too pushy, try it anyway, if for nothing other than the experience. You've really got nothing to lose. And there's nothing terrifying or offensive about coffee except for the caffeine. It's likely that he'd love to join you, and will appreciate your initiative. Remember that the worst thing that can happen isn't so terrible: If he says no, then you have a much-needed additional half hour to yourself. And if he says that he'd like to but has to be somewhere else in a few minutes, consider giving him your business card and suggest that you get together another time. Take down his number as well.

You might find it easiest to approach someone you've seen repeatedly as opposed to a man you're meeting for the first time, but don't miss an opportunity. In boldness, there's genius—and potential for great times.

▲▲▲

The Shy Person's Guide to Party-Going

1. Remember that you'll never see these people again—unless you choose to.
2. Wear something that you think you look great in.
3. Before you arrive, think of a few anecdotes you enjoy telling, or some questions you might ask either to start a conversation or to keep one going.
4. Promise yourself that you'll stay for at least a certain amount of time.
5. Remember people's names when you're introduced to them. (Sometimes it helps to think of a mnemonic, or simply repeat the name to yourself after the person says it. You'll make an impression if you remember the person's name later that evening or a few weeks later when your paths cross again.)
6. Figure out the location of the bathrooms, phones, etc., in case you need to escape from a fading conversation. It's also fine to say something like "I've enjoyed talking to you. See you later."
7. Take the long route to get yourself a drink and wander around the room.
8. Talk to the person selling tickets, serving drinks, passing hors d'oeuvres.
9. Ask someone to dance.
10. Suppress your first instinct to leave. Give it another five minutes.
11. When all else fails, head for the bowl of pretzels. (You're sure to find company there.)

▼▼▼

First, Old Friends

*Is it possible, on such a sudden, you
should fall into so strong a liking . . . ?*
   —Celia, in Shakespeare's
   As You Like It

*I have noticed before that there is a category of
acquaintance that is not friendship or business or
romance, but speculation, fascination.*
   —Jane Smiley

As you begin planning your efforts to meet interesting men,
don't forget about a potentially promising source of new guys
to date: old friends (or Friends—see sidebar on p. 87).

Try visualization. Think of the single men you enjoy spending time with. Can you see yourself in a different sort of relationship with any of them? Perhaps the basis for friendship can
be the foundation for something else. There's comfort in dating someone you already know and feel at ease with; you get to

skip some of the preliminaries. Of course, shifting a friendship into something amorous can have its own awkward moments, but they're fleeting.

The good news is that chances are pretty great if you sense a possible romantic connection with a friend that the feelings are mutual. That thing called chemistry is probably in the air. Give it room to expand. Let the suppressed attraction surface. Feel free to flirt, and then follow up.

How to do this? Be bold. The straightforward approach might be best. If he lives nearby, suggest that it would be nice to get together for dinner. Choose a place that's slightly nicer than the places you and he usually frequent together, and before you finish your meal, speak candidly about your feelings. If he lives out of town, invite him to visit, or go see him. Tell him, in whatever words feel right for you, that you've been thinking a lot lately about your friendship, and wonder about switching gears. You'll be able to sense from his immediate reaction whether you want to continue the conversation. If he responds positively, the two of you can figure out the rest.

If he's not open to your suggestion, it might be because there are other things in his life at that moment that you aren't aware of. Or that he simply prefers to remain friends. No harm done; although you might feel momentary embarrassment, you'll get back on track quickly. You can even make a joke about having watched *When Harry Met Sally* too many times. It's likely that the conversation will deepen the friendship, not hurt it.

It's not unusual that old friends evolve into boyfriends. Although it can happen naturally, more often one person needs to take action to refashion a relationship. Go for it. It's worth the risk. You'll both be pleased.

▲▲

Naming "Him" (or How to Describe or Introduce Him to Friends and Family)

1. A date: You've met him; the jury is still out.
2. This guy: They've heard you talk about him before.

3. My Friend: Capital *F*. Somewhere between date and boyfriend.
4. My Old Friend: Capital *F*. We still haven't resolved what this is.
5. My buddy: A friend (lowercase) for life—a.k.a. pal.
6. My escort: He's the man who agreed to use my extra ticket when the date/guy/Friend backed out.
7. My boyfriend: There's a future here, maybe. Single friends should cease flirting with him.
8. My beau: Boyfriend, for those who spent their junior year in Paris.
9. My lover: Same as above. You might try a different term with parents.
10. My companion/spouse-equivalent/significant other: The one and only.

▼▼▼

First Phone Calls

Questions are never indiscreet. Answers sometimes are.

> —Mrs. Cheveley, in Oscar
> Wilde's *An Ideal Husband*

It would be interesting to know what it is men are most afraid of. Taking a new step, uttering a new word.

> —Fyodor Dostoevski

Telephone connections can be key to romantic connections. In fact, telephones, and especially answering machines, are indispensable to dating. If you're curious about a certain man, you can get clues about him by looking up his phone number and listening to his message (when he's not home). You'll learn if he lives alone, and can also get a sense of his personality—whether he's businesslike, informal, chatty, funny, gruff—through the tone and content of his message and the sound of his voice.

Thanks to these now ubiquitous machines, you can rehearse your lines and leave perfect-sounding messages, screen phone calls, retrieve messages left on your machine when you're expecting (hoping) someone will call you back, and save certain messages so that you can listen to the voices again.

He Calls You First: Blind Dates

You answer your telephone to hear an unknown man's voice ask for you, mispronouncing your name. Before you cut short what you assume is a fund-raising sales pitch, remember that your aunt/decorator/literary agent promised to give your phone number to her new colleague, and this might be him. You can let him go through his full explanation of the lineage of your connection—or you can politely cut him off and say you know exactly who he is and are very pleased to hear from him. (Some aunts neglect to let you know when they give out your number. If the call takes you by surprise, it's just as well not to let him know that, for his anxiety level is high at the moment, too. Once you've subtly determined—as best you can—that the connection is legitimate, let him know that you appreciate his calling.)

Be friendly, ask some questions about him, laugh, and keep the conversation brief—and directed toward making a plan to meet. It can be really frustrating to spend an hour on one of these calls and hang up without having made a date. You don't want to be scrutinized, as though you were applying for a job, or cross-examined, as though you were an accomplice in crime, on the phone. And, you don't want to let yourself do too much judging based on the phone call. Some people who aren't great on the phone are terrific in person.

This is not to say that if a man talks nonstop about his interest in insects that you must meet him (unless, of course, you share that interest). However, do try to be open. If he doesn't bring up getting together early into the call, you can propose that you continue the conversation in person sometime. The best of these introductory calls are short, upbeat, and polite, and they achieve their goal: you have a date.

▲▲▲

Male Voices II

Eli, a New Jersey doctor: "If you're interested in a man, make yourself available. If you look at your date book and say that you're not free for two weeks, I assume you just weren't interested."

Len, a New York investor: "Don't wear a Walkman while working out at the gym if you want to meet men. A Walkman is worse than a wedding band. If you want men to talk to you, wear a T-shirt with some writing on it. The name of a place or a slogan can be a conversation opener. One last thing: Ask the man reading on the machine next to yours if you can borrow a section of his newspaper."

Joe, a Washington banker: "It's really acceptable—and appreciated—when a woman takes initiative. If I show some interest in someone, I'm pleased when she takes the next step. My advice: Don't wait around."

Bill, a New York radio producer: "I see women who look like they'd like to start a conversation, but they hold back. Here's what I suggest: Don't be inhibited. Don't be afraid that a man will get the wrong idea, that is, assuming that you're not in a hotel bar, but in some neutral territory. Make a comment—about anything. If the guy is too stupid to pick up on it, you don't want to go out with him anyway."

Josh, a New York advertising executive: "If a woman has questions about a guy she's dating—if she doesn't understand his actions, or is trying to figure out what he's thinking—she should ask another man for advice. It makes more sense to turn to a male friend or a brother than to her girlfriends, who won't really understand either."

▼▼▼

If he calls at your office and it's inconvenient to talk then, let him know that you'd be happy to talk at some other time. Suggest a few possible times that he might reach you, and get his phone number too. If you don't hear from him after those suggested times pass, you might call him and say that you know you've been difficult to reach for the past few days and wanted to get back to him.

If he calls and gets your answering machine instead of you, he's likely to leave a message explaining the connection. Call back promptly, at your convenience. If you get his machine, leave a friendly message instructing him when and where to best reach you. Try to do your best to avoid an extended game of telephone tag: You both might lose interest in the connection.

The same advice applies if you run a personal ad and get responses by phone, or if someone calls after receiving your note about their ad, albeit with a slight twist. The men mentioned above—who either got your name through someone you know or met you before—have been screened in some way. If someone calls and sounds truly strange or annoying, it's okay to put aside your vow of openness. Say no, or end the conversation before he has the opportunity to ask you for a date. But do be direct. It's more unkind than you think to tell someone you're busy and suggest he try again when you have no intention of dating him.

A tested principle to follow: If the caller has someone else's stamp of approval, that is, he's calling at the suggestion of an individual you're connected to, do your best to meet him, for two reasons. First, you never know, and you have nothing to lose except a little time. Second, if someone thinks well enough of you to do a generous favor for you, it's best not to let that person down by backing out of your role in the deal, which is simply to meet the man. More important, if this particular match isn't an inspired idea, perhaps the next one will be, and you do want your cousin/colleague/neighbor to keep fine-tuning those matchmaking skills.

However, if the caller is totally unknown and his call arrives out of the blue, you might be more cautious. But try not to be too picky before you give the man a chance.

▲▲

Meg: . . . In a place like New York, people meet people all the time.

Ruby: Not eligible males.

Meg: What I mean, most girls fall in love with someone in the neighborhood. And New York is a pretty big neighborhood.

Heidi: As far as I'm concerned, living here is like going to an all-girl college.

Meg: I just came from an all-girl college.

Heidi: No!

Meg: Four years. I live in a tiny town with a tremendous college for girls.

Ruby: You poor kid.

Meg: Getting a date was like winning the Irish Sweepstakes.

Heidi: I'm afraid you came to the wrong place.

Meg: Where *should* I have gone?

Ada: A western mining town. I hear there are ten men for every girl.

Meg: I've bought clothes—told everyone—and they all expect—I have to get a job, make a success, write glowing letters home about all the things I'm doing.

Heidi: Lots of luck.

Ruby: When you've finished with the letters, you better write a book. We'll all buy copies.

—from *Ask Any Girl*, adapted by Christopher Sergel
from the book by Winifred Wolfe

▼▼

First Calls From People You've Met

No, this doesn't only happen in fairy tales. The interesting man you met while on vacation or at a neighborhood meeting may find your telephone number in the phone book and call you directly. And all three men to whom you gave your business cards at a holiday party might promptly get in touch. Second only to finding a half-price label on the dress you've been eyeing, getting those calls is a great lift, whether expected or not, unless you're certain that you don't care to spend another minute with the guy. And don't be so sure. Give him some credit for calling. Remember, be open.

If you've already spent time getting acquainted in person, you might spend a little more time conversing on the phone than in the blind date situation, that is, if you like speaking on the telephone. If not, you can let the man know that you can't stay on the phone and try to arrange to meet. No matter how long you are on the telephone, try not to hang up without having a specific plan for getting together. Either one or both of you might have a busy schedule, upcoming travel, or major deadlines. Try to make a date anyway, even if it's a few weeks ahead and might have to be rescheduled. Let him know that your plans might change unexpectedly but you will do your best to make it. Far better to have to reschedule a date than not to have one to change.

You Call Him

Even the experts on etiquette are easing up on this one: It really is fine for women to call men. If you think of yourself as old-fashioned, confine this instinct to choosing vintage clothing or antique furnishings; don't let it hold you back from making a phone call. You should replace the notion that women can't call men with an expanded list of telephone numbers. Take a deep breath, dial. Speak cheerfully. You'll feel great afterward, especially if you get his answering machine and can leave a message for him to call back.

Glenn O'Brien, writing in *Playboy*, advises women: "Not only is it OK for a woman to ask a man for a date, I think it's necessary. Not all the time, but some of the time. If women can fly military aircraft, they can also call me up for a date." Even if your only association with military matters is watching Goldie Hawn in *Private Benjamin*, keep his words in mind.

If you're nervous about making the call, think of what you'll say ahead of time. Play out the exchange in your mind, think of topics to discuss, and even jot down a few notes. But be prepared to put aside your script as the conversation rolls ahead, for he won't have the same script in front of him.

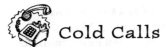 ## Cold Calls

When you hear that your out-of-town sister's neighbor is moving to your city, call and welcome him to town. See if you can help with any practical advice. It's important that you trust your instincts; it's fine to extend yourself to potential dates in the same way you would to potential friends. Invite him for a drink or coffee—just as you would if he were a she. See what develops. Or if you learn that a terrific friend of a friend is available but shy about calling you, get his number and call him first. No doubt he'll appreciate your effort. Suggest the drinks or coffee routine. You have nothing—*nothing*—to lose.

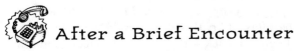 ## After a Brief Encounter

Sure, you would prefer that the man you exchange business cards with at a conference send you a bouquet the following day with a note inviting you to dinner. Or you wouldn't mind a late-night phone call, without the flowers. But don't waste your time hoping that he'll call, lamenting that he hasn't, or waiting for the telephone to ring. Perhaps he lost your card and can't remember your last name. Call him. Say that you really enjoyed meeting him and would like to continue the conversation and perhaps you can meet for coffee. Or if you're feeling more bold, suggest that you go and see the new film you were discussing. For the not yet bold, your relief is the telephone answering machine, which may just have been invented so that women can leave messages for men they'd like to have call them back. Find a time that he's unlikely to be at home; leave a message reminding him of your pleasant meeting and suggest a get-together. Don't forget to leave your phone number. Be prepared for his call back by rereading "First Calls From People You've Met," on page 94.

▲▲▲

Stress-Reduced Methods for Asking Men Out

1. "I have an extra ticket for a screening of a new film/baseball game/concert and was wondering if you might be free to join me." (After he says yes, borrow or buy the tickets.)
2. "Would you like to grab a cup of coffee after class tonight/next week/before the lecture/right now?" (Have in mind a nice place to go.)
3. "Some friends are coming over to watch the football game/election debate/movie. Would you like to join us?" (Then invite friends. Consider asking a married couple.)
4. "I'm thinking of seeing the new film/exhibition/building complex. Are you interested in going sometime?" (After he says yes, agree on a time.)
5. "Do you play tennis/play golf/cycle? I'm always looking for new partners." (Try this only if you're athletic. If you're a beginner, stick with coffee and concerts for now.)
6. Pass your business card to him with a note on the back saying, "Let me know if you'd like to meet for lunch."

▼▼

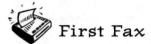 **First Fax**

A date invitation by fax? Not unheard of, and quite efficient for busy people who are hard to reach. Feel free to respond by fax or phone. Remember, if the fax is in his office, his might not be the only eyes reading your note.

First Dates

It is a truth universally acknowledged that a single man in possession of a good fortune must be in want of a wife.
—Jane Austen

The future was plump with promise.
—Maya Angelou

Thoughts of dating can make grown-ups feel like they're in junior high school again. If you feel like you are sixteen at age twenty-eight or even forty-eight, be grateful for the burst of youthfulness—and that this time you don't have to ask your parents' permission or be home in time for curfew. Anthropologists may say dating is a ritual; it's also a skill to be developed. For some, it's a favorite hobby.

A first date is a tryout. Both sides are checking out the other, subtly investigating whether this new person will fit into their dreams. It's an evening (or afternoon) full of possibility and promise. You can present your absolutely best side and take delight in your date's interest in everything about you. You can ask (almost) any question you're interested in knowing about him. Perhaps there'll be mutual attraction, even magic. Or maybe you'll be thrilled if he's simply a nice guy.

Try to enjoy this interval of dating while it lasts. Your married friends will be envious of your adventures, and will vicariously experience the moments of high drama (and despair too, if that is the case). Your grandchildren will enjoy hearing your tales again and again.

You may be used to going out in groups, in which your male and female friends make plans together as to what movie to see or whose living room to congregate in. A date—one woman and one man—requires a choreography all its own. The first steps are about decision making—when to meet, where to go, who pays.

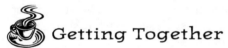 Getting Together

Keep it public. If you've met the guy through the personals, or know very little about him, please don't have him pick you up at your home. Caution is essential. Not to worry you, but your safety is very important. So don't take unnecessary risks. Meet him at a very public place *you've* selected. Even if you know him through friends, for your first actual meeting you might prefer to travel to your meeting place on your own. When your car is parked outside (or if you can easily flag down a taxi or walk home), you have a certain freedom. You can leave whenever you wish or stay as long as you want. Knowing that, you can arrive with assurance and depart with safety.

Choose a very specific place to meet. If you're going to a restaurant, clarify if you'll be inside or outside; if you're meeting at a museum, specify which entrance. Be on time. No need for grand entrances. No one enjoys being kept waiting.

Once you've made plans, be sure to get his telephone number in case your schedule changes. If you're curious to know where he lives and he hasn't told you, consult the telephone book. You can match up his number and address—and find out if he lives with his parents.

Don't hang up without asking, "How will I recognize you?" You'll need to share basic information about height, hair color, or any easily identifiable quality, but there's no need for too many details. Be prepared to be amused by how imprecise people can be in their self-descriptions: A man five-foot-eight might describe himself as tall; a balding man might say he has blond hair.

▲▲▲

Bad Choices for First Dates:

1. Noisy restaurants or bars—unless you know sign language.
2. His mother's for dinner.
3. Your mother's for dessert.
4. Romantic movies. (Whether you think you like the guy or not, watching passionate kissing scenes while sitting next to him can feel uncomfortable.)
5. A singles-only event.
6. The opening of your favorite store's once-a-year blowout sale.

▼▼▼

First Date Possibilities

Sitting down face to face over some sort of food and/or beverage, whether it's a cup of tea or a multicourse dinner, is the most common—and jovial—way to get acquainted. It may also be the most time-efficient. You'll learn a lot about the man from your conversation, the lively moments and the silent pauses, and from his manners, how he treats you and deals with the waiters. And keep an eye on the body language generated between you. Breaking bread together can build ties.

Other activities, like long walks and museum visits, also can be conducive to good communication. But if you're more comfortable with less talk the first time out, that's fine. Think about going to a movie, concert, or hockey game (as long as you both enjoy the game). You'll spend most of your time together sitting adjacent to one another, looking straight ahead, and you'll be able to pick up some clues from the shoulder that might be touching yours. You will also have plenty to talk about from the action in front of you or the scenery that's unfolding before you.

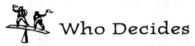 ## Who Decides

Good manners prescribe that the person who does the inviting selects the place or activity. You already know that men vary in their approach, based on their sense of what's appropriate, which has little to do with age, income level, or ethnic background, but is related to lessons likely learned from their mothers (something to keep in mind in raising sons who'll date smart women). Be prepared for every possibility when the man is doing the inviting. It can be anything from a formal request that you go to a specific place at a specific time for a specific event, an open-ended invitation that requires your input and approval, or the whole matter could be left in your hands.

When you extend the invitation, you can design the logistics to best suit you or the situation. You may also choose to let your new acquaintance decide what you'll do together.

In many situations, the question of inviter/invitee is not relevant. The decision to meet is mutually agreed on. Whatever the situation, keep in mind an earlier lesson: You're in control. Be as flexible and easygoing as you wish, or assert your will in a friendly way. It's a matter of personal style.

If the plans he suggests aren't to your liking, make an alternate suggestion. If he invites you to join him at his company's dinner dance as a first date and you'd rather meet over drinks, tell him the truth: that you wouldn't feel comfortable at a party where you don't know anyone, and you'd prefer that the two of you had the opportunity to get acquainted first. Or if he suggests dinner and you want to keep the first encounter shorter (maybe), tell another truth: that you don't want to put off getting together but that you're extremely busy at work and that right now it would be better to meet earlier in the evening for a drink. Feel free to propose a meeting place on your side of town (tell him that you prefer to be in your neighborhood) if you don't like the one he suggests, and if he doesn't like your suggestion, come up with an alternate choice. You can make sure everything—the place, the day, the time—is just fine for you.

To be prepared for these first date calls, it's a good idea to keep in mind a checklist of favorite places—a café with ambiance, a quiet bar, a cozy restaurant. Be familiar with choices in various neighborhoods, and be sure to know their full names, addresses, and any significant directions. You can have your way, and if you have the information to back it up, your resourcefulness will be appreciated. That way you won't have to go through the "I don't know, where do you want to go?" routine.

 ## Best Places

Your objective is to get to know this potentially interesting man. That's best accomplished in pleasant surroundings.

In selecting a site to sit and eat or drink, think of the place's atmosphere, and how comfortable you might feel there. Avoid bright lighting (everyone looks more attractive in softer lighting), loud or crowded spaces (even if you find that you don't agree with any of his opinions, you should be able to hear what he says), and restaurants that are too obviously romantic spots (save that for a later date).

Every bar, pub, coffee shop, restaurant has a distinctive mood, although some might be hard to classify; match the mood you think you'd like for the date with that of a place. For a casual drink, go to a local pub. Take in a long afternoon of conversation over a bottomless cup of coffee at a European café. For a lively meal with lots of color, try a little-known ethnic joint you've just discovered. Enjoy a businesslike get-acquainted drink in the bar of a grand hotel.

When you're selecting a restaurant, consider the price range, and avoid places that are very expensive. There's no need for a first meeting to require a major financial investment. See page 107 to clarify the question of who pays, but in any case, the first date shouldn't cost an excessive amount of money. However, if the man calls and invites you to be his guest for dinner at a specific restaurant—and you know it happens to be an expensive place—feel free to accept. He might be trying hard to impress you, and you're correct to assume that he'll pay.

 ## Foodless Dates

You don't have to be fasting to prefer spending conversational time that doesn't revolve around eating. You can sit undisturbed in hotel lobbies, public parks and gardens, and shopping malls. Some buildings have striking atriums open to the public.

You can also walk though the zoo, wander about the grounds of an old mansion, explore an out-of-the-way neighborhood, window-shop along major avenues, visit art galleries, conduct your own walking tour of historic sites, or stroll along the shore or boardwalk.

Watch something interesting together—and then you have a ready subject for conversation afterward. Go to a movie; old classics can be great fun. Attend the theater, symphony, or jazz concert. If you decide to attend a lecture, be certain to choose a subject of mutual interest.

For something unusual, try night court. Sit in the spectators' section, and it can be better than having orchestra seats to a Broadway show.

Think transportation. Ride the ferry or tram. Board a double-decker bus. Go for a drive along country lanes. My sister loved to go with her dates to the airport; they'd wander through the international terminal and gaze at families reuniting and those saying good-bye, browse in the duty-free shops, and find a corner to watch takeoffs and landings.

Consider noncompetitive sports. Rent roller-blades. Go for a bicycle ride. Try miniature golf. If you're self-confident in a bathing suit, enjoy the sun together at the beach or local pool.

Be a spectator. Watch the ice skaters. Head for the racetrack. Get tickets for a tennis match or basketball game. It can be great fun to watch Little League baseball or soccer, even if you don't know the players. And then you might cap a pleasant time with something to eat or drink wherever you end up.

Time of Day

Experiment. Evening dates are the most common. You might also enjoy meeting someone on a weekend afternoon. Think about high tea. Morning people might prefer early tennis games and breakfast. Try an afternoon movie when you can avoid the crowds.

Some women prefer meeting first dates over lunch during the week. For them, the issue of time efficiency is most important. Only a limited, previously agreed on amount of time is spent as both people need to return to their offices, and worries over saying good-night are moot. It's not the most relaxed setting, but it works, especially for busy people. Keep in mind when selecting a restaurant that you don't want to be at a place where your colleagues—and former lunch dates—are likely to be.

What to Wear

The most important advice is to wear something that *you* like. Think of an outfit that's comfortable, that doesn't need much fussing. You don't want to be pulling at the front of your dress to make sure it's covering or uncovering as you intended, and you don't even want to think about the possibility of sinking shoulder pads or dangling slips. Dress as you please. If all black is your signature, go for it. But if you're concerned about being too formal or informal, go for the middle ground. Some men will give you an indication of how they'll be dressed when they make plans with you, and you might want to make your decision accordingly.

If you're the type of person who needs to try on every outfit you own before going out, it's best to decide what you'll wear beforehand so that you're not still changing when it's time to leave.

▲▲

What Not to Wear on a First Date

1. A jumpsuit—or anything that will take you twenty minutes to reassemble when you excuse yourself to go to the bathroom.
2. The heart-shaped locket given to you by your ex-boyfriend/husband.
3. High heels, if you're uncertain of his height and will be uncomfortable if you stand a head taller than him.
4. Your favorite tailored suit—if you're going for a stroll in the park on a weekend afternoon.
5. Gym shorts and a sweatshirt—if you're meeting for drinks at a five-star hotel.
6. An outfit that looks like it might have been designed by Madonna.
7. A sweater dress that makes you itch all over.

▼▼

Moment of Encounter/ Moment of Truth

A good predate exercise is to visualize a couple you know who seem well suited, and focus on those aspects of their relationship that you admire, and also on how you would feel to be a partner in such a positive match. Then, stage an inner pep rally and you'll be ready.

In all cases of men you meet through personal ads or through indirect contacts, simply don't waver from the rule of meeting them for the first time in a public space. If he's the son of your uncle's best friend—and you're absolutely sure he's not a potential murderer—and you've agreed to have him pick you up at your home, you might be able to get a peek of him through your window or keyhole before you open the door and face him. If you live in an apartment building, you can meet in the lobby or entranceway—you don't have to buzz him into the building. Understand that telephone voices and other peoples' descriptions can be deceiving; you may be in for a large surprise, for better and worse. No matter; be open.

When you don't have the advantage of a keyhole preview, it's still simple to identify a date you haven't met before. There's a certain aura that people about to embark on a blind date project—a combination of awkwardness, anticipation, and anxiety. You can usually spot the other person trying to search the room inconspicuously. Once you find the man who appears to be your intended date, you can approach him and greet him in a friendly manner, asking if he is Mike or Brian or Phillip, or whoever you are to meet. Or he might approach you first.

I know a woman who walked up to a good-looking man who seemed to fit the description of the man she was to meet, and asked if he was her date. "I'm not but I'd like to be," he said, and asked if they might go out together the following evening. After exchanging business cards, they agreed to meet in the same place. She then found the man she was supposed to meet and had a miserable time, but she returned the next night and began a terrific relationship with the man she'd mistaken for her date.

▲▲

What Not to Discuss on the First Date . . . Unless You're Asked

1. The *M* word: *marriage.*
2. The *C* word: *commitment.*
3. Your ex-boyfriend/husband's bad habits.
4. Your ex's mother.
5. Your chronic dry skin problem.
6. The stain on his tie.
7. The three other dates you have—or turned down—that week.
8. Where you'd rather be at that moment.

▼▼

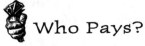 ## Who Pays?

Tradition reigns, but as with most aspects of modern-day dating, there are no immutable rules. Do understand that money-related issues can be tangled, involving questions of power and expectations as well as dollars and cents.

At least on the first date, most men will pick up the tab. Even if you extend the invitation, they're likely to reach for the check first. If you're uncomfortable with that, offer to pay your share. Many men will decline the suggestion (although they appreciate it), but insist if you feel it is important. Or, if you're in a restaurant, offer to leave the tip, or pay for the movie if he pays for dinner. You can also thank him graciously and let him know that next time it's your treat (and that's one way of letting him know that you're interested in going out again). It's also fine to let him keep paying for everything. If you're dating a student, you might feel more inclined to share expenses than if you're with a corporate executive. Do what's most comfortable for you.

If you want to flash a message that "this isn't really a date and we're really just friends," demand to pay your share. But don't be surprised if he doesn't get it. Many men are also puzzled about how to deal with this issue, and out of fear of offending a date will allow a woman—who might not really want to pay but offers—to pay.

I once offered to split a dinner bill (out of politeness, not conviction), and my date whipped out a calculator in order to figure out our shares according to what we each ordered. No surprise, he was an accountant. I made sure to give him the correct number of pennies, and knew the evening would make for a great story, but not much else.

▲▲▲

What Not to Order on a First Date in a Restaurant:
1. The most expensive thing on the menu.
2. Frogs' legs, calves' brains, pigs' knuckles, or any body part that resembles a biology lab specimen—or any food that makes kids squeal.
3. Linguini—or any pasta that requires twirling unless you're a pro—with marinara sauce.
4. General Ho's One-Hundred Garlic Chicken—unless your date is having at least half as many cloves.
5. "Just water" if your date is ordering dinner.
6. Dinner if your date is ordering "just water"—time to leave.

▼▼▼

What if You're Not Sure if It's a D-A-T-E?

It's not uncommon to spend time alone with a male friend or colleague. But what happens if it's suddenly clear, as you're finishing dinner, that there's something more in the air than friendship? Unless the man facing you is a work colleague with whom a relationship at that moment could be problematic, be candid. With a touch of irony, ask if the evening has been a date, and see how he responds. If you're not comfortable being so bold, wait out a few more quasi-romantic dinners, and then ask. Chances are quite good that he's just as interested—potentially—as you are. (See Chapter 7.)

Great Escapes

After your date introduces himself, if you feel your heart sink to your toes, try to resist the impulse to say that he has mistaken you for someone else. You've already come this far; give the guy a chance. Set a minimum time requirement—forty-five minutes is fair—and try to stick to it. You can always excuse yourself earlier than planned if you're convinced that you'd rather be scrubbing your bathroom tiles than spending another minute with your date. There's no need, however, to tell him that.

There's the headache approach ("I've got to run—I feel one of my migraines coming on") or the honesty-is-the-best policy style ("I think you're a fine person but I don't see any potential for a future relationship here so I'd like to save us both the time and trouble"). Or you can make sure that your meal lands in your lap. Your dry cleaner will understand.

Whatever your preferred escape routine, if you have to activate it, be courteous. You might be tempted to excuse yourself for the bathroom and never return, but that's heartless. Understand that in cases of blind dates, your matchmaker will probably hear about it. You may want to reach that person soon after—before your date does—and express your appreciation for his or her efforts no matter what the outcome, explain your reactions, and offer some guidelines about what you're looking for, in the hope that this matchmaker will try again.

▲▲▲

Date Predicaments: To Tell or Not?

1. *You've been together for a few hours and can't remember his name.* Ask if he has any nicknames. If that doesn't work, ask how he spells his name—and hope that it isn't Bob.

2. *Your former boyfriend and a date are being escorted to the next table.* Pray that your ex will notice you before getting any closer and ask for a different table. If not, call the maitre d' and explain your problem. He'll gracefully move one of you. If you don't want to tell your date the whole truth, tell half: that you're uncomfortable because the woman is a business colleague and you don't want her to overhear your conversation. (The true half is that you're uncomfortable.)

3. *His toupee is off center and perilously close to falling off.* He doesn't notice. Best to say nothing.

4. *You've already seen the show he's arranged to get tickets for.* Two choices: If it's clear that he's gone to some trouble and you don't mind seeing it again, say nothing. But if you can't bear to see it again, explain. Thank him for his efforts, and suggest that he go with another friend to the show, and that you'll meet him another time. Don't feel guilty. He should have checked with you first.

5. *You're at a black-tie dinner and the back of your near-backless dress is splitting.* Yes, explain. Ask to borrow his jacket. Check for safety pins in the ladies' room. If you can't salvage it, keep the jacket on.

6. *At the end of a pleasant evening, he asks if he can come up for a drink. You know that if you invite him in, it might be difficult to get him to leave, and you don't want to deal with that—yet.* Tell him you have a house guest (name her, so that he realizes it's a female) and you're afraid of disturbing her. (You can find a half-truth in that.) Or, say that you're in the middle of spring cleaning and the place is a total mess. You'd like him to see it when it's back in order.

7. *He takes you to his boss's home for dinner and when you get there*

you realize that she is the ex-wife of your favorite cousin, whom she dumped. Try to be pleasant. When you have a moment alone with your date, tell him—and then continue the nice act.

8. *You're on a double date with a friend, and you're more attracted to her date than yours. You think the feeling is mutual.* Wait until the following day and find out if she is interested in the guy. If not, feel free to call him. If she likes him, do nothing, for now. But, if he calls you . . .

9. *You and a date go to the movies and you see another man you're dating with a group of male friends.* Wave to him and be friendly. Try not to appear embarrassed. Perhaps he'll think you're with your brother.

▼▼

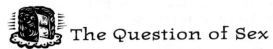 The Question of Sex

I leave that one to you. Some women feel that they're doing everything wrong in this area. My advice: Do what's comfortable for you. Both initial chastity and casual sex are commonplace. It's fine to take your time, and then take more time, if you wish. Your date might feel as awkward as you do. Signs and signals can be misinterpreted when you don't know someone well, so you may want to be direct—after the first date, or after an interval of dating, whenever you're ready—about wanting to move ahead.

Happy Endings (or How to Let Him Know That You'd Like to Do This Again)

Tell him that you're really pleased to have met him, and that you'd like to get together again. Feel free to say that you're sometimes reluctant to go on blind dates, but that you're really glad he called. That you'll have to thank the person who introduced you. That you'd like him to come over for dinner. That you really enjoy his company. That you look forward to getting to know him. That you had a fabulous evening. The rest—how you want to orchestrate the rest of the ending (or beginning)— is up to you.

A male friend of mine who is newly single and enjoying dating is definitive about what turns him off at the end of a date: when women press him to make a definite plan to get together again, or interrogate him to find out if he'll go out with them again. What he doesn't understand is that what he perceives as aggressiveness grows out of many women's repeated experiences of men promising to call and not following through. Still, his reactions can be instructive. Even if you prefer that everything be perfectly clear at the end of a date, try not to steamroll ahead. You'll need to accept the fact that all aspects of dating are full of ambiguity. But feel free to call in a few days. In fact, this same man says he appreciates when women don't wait for him to call first.

Other Endings

If you're certain you'd be pleased never to see him again, thank him and wish him good luck. Decline his offer to see you home. If you're not sure how you feel, take the more positive tack, described above. You never know. Mediocre first dates can generate glorious seconds and thirds.

10

First Things to Do Next

*All human wisdom is summed up in two words:
wait and hope.*

—Alexandre Dumas

*If you never want to see a man again, say, "I
love you. I want to marry you. I want to have
children"—they leave skid marks.*

—Rita Rudner

$\mathcal{U}$niversally, women despise when men say they'll call and don't. "Why say it if they don't mean it? It would be better if they said nothing at all." I agree, and would like to patent a pocket lie detector shield that could be pointed at a date when he promises to call. A lie would set off a silent alarm alerting a nearby pigeon to do her thing above his head. Justice would be served.

Clearly, it would be wonderful if all men called the next day to say they enjoyed your company and were thinking of you, and would love to see you again very soon. Those who do get extra credit. Some men intend to call you and indeed will do so—but it might take them ten days or two weeks or longer.

▲▲
When to Skip the Second Date:
1. You call him back to confirm the place you'd planned to meet and the female voice on his answering machine—clearly not his mother's—informs you that "we're not home now."
2. You see him slip a ring into his pants pocket while he is waiting for you.
3. You see him slip the silverware into his overcoat pocket as you are leaving the restaurant.
4. He tells you that he wants to marry someone exactly like his mother.
5. He uses his cellular phone during dinner to confirm his date for the following evening.

▼▼

 **Timing**

Forget those rules you may vaguely remember about a man's obligation to call no later than Wednesday for a Saturday night date. It's really fine if he calls on Thursday or later. But if you don't like the fact that he's calling Saturday afternoon to find out what you're doing that evening, tell him you'd like to see him but you're busy (even if your plan is to wash your hair) and arrange to get together sometime soon.

You also need to recognize that whether a man calls you after a first date or not might have nothing to do with you. You can't learn everything that's going on in his life after one date. He might have been genuinely thrilled to have met you and meant every kind word he said—but the next day he heard from his ex-girlfriend that she wanted to get back together, or from his boss that he was being transferred abroad, or from his doctor that he needed surgery. It would be considerate if he called anyway to let you know that, but don't count on it.

What to Do When He Doesn't Call

Call him. No doubt he'll be pleased to hear from you. Ask him if he'd like to see that new show you discussed. Invite him to join you at a concert you have tickets for (and then go buy the tickets). Or just call him to chat and tell him that you wanted to thank him again for a lovely evening. He'll probably beat you to the question of whether you'd like to get together again, but if he doesn't, ask him. Why not?

If you're reticent about calling, experiment with other forms of communication. Think of these gestures as prelove letters. Send a note or a picture postcard (try either a museum art card or a tourist photo that relates to something mentioned when you met) with a brief message about how you enjoyed meeting him and look forward to seeing him again. Or, enclose a newspaper or magazine article that you think will interest him and note "in case you missed this." Getting mail from you will remind him to call, which he meant to do.

A friend who works for a major publishing firm has a tried-and-true method for getting men to live up to their promise of calling. She has the advantage of a stockroom of books at her disposal. Her routine is to send the man a book with a friendly note tucked inside, saying that she thought he'd be interested in this particular title. The odds are pretty high that within days he'll call to thank her and ask to go out with her again.

▲▲▲

**Discreet Ways to Ask the Toughest Questions
(how to find out your date's age and other facts
you need to know)**

1. *Age:* Find out where he went to college, and then try to place the decade and draw out some details that might provide some clues about his year of graduation. "Oh, you went to Yale. So did my brother. Any overlap with the Clintons?"

2. *Previous marriages:* Direct can be discreet too. "Have you ever been married before?"

3. *Children:* Likewise. "Do you have kids?" (Or, if you're not so comfortable with the straight-arrow approach: "Do you like children?")

4. *Living arrangements:* Do you enjoy living alone? (He might not admit to a live-in girlfriend he's thinking of leaving, but if you sense some discomfort in his answer, he may not be as unattached as he'd like you to believe . . . or he might live with his parents.)

5. *Religion:* (In springtime) "Will you do something special for Easter/Passover?" (You can vary the question based on the season and your hunch of what holiday he might celebrate.)

6. *General health:* "Do you belong to a gym?" Or tell him that you're fed up with the medical system and find out his opinion.

7. *Financial solvency:* Try a combination of direct ("How long have you been at your job? What did you do before?") and indirect questions ("Have you ever been to Las Vegas?"). You can make certain inferences from his clothing, but you can't be too sure. He might have borrowed the Armani suit he's wearing.

▼▼▼

What to Do If He Calls Too Often

Murphy's law dictates that this only happens when you're not interested.

If it's a sure thing that you never want to see him again, it's best to be clear—and kind—when he calls. No need for details. You don't need to remind him that he repeated the same story several times over dinner, or that he finished all the food on your plate without asking if you were done. Some women worry about hurting men's feelings by turning them down too bluntly and prefer to invent business trips, floors that needs frequent washing, sudden illness, and endless meetings. It's more considerate to be straightforward, rather than keeping him dangling when there's less chance that you'd go out with him again than you'd let your five-year-old niece give you a haircut.

Be honest, or close to it. It's not easy to spurn someone gracefully. Tell him that you enjoyed the opportunity to get to know him but you don't think it would work in the long run. If you prefer to be vague, say that the timing isn't right just now. Or that you thought you were ready for a new relationship but you realize that you're not. The downside of the vague approach is that he might be encouraged and call you back some weeks later to check if you're "ready."

Before you hang up, there's one last thing you might do. Unless he's truly bad news, think about introducing him to another single woman you know. Remember that someone who strikes you as dull might be sparkling to someone else. Tell him that although things didn't work out between the two of you, you think highly of him and have a sense that he'd enjoy meeting a friend of yours, and that you'd be happy to arrange that. He's likely to feel flattered, even if a bit rejected, and will appreciate your honesty as well as your suggestion. If he's willing to call, check with your friend (follow the advice in Chapter 3), and get back to him with her number. You're doing everyone a favor.

▲▲
Sure Signs That Your Foreign-accented Suitor Is After a Visa

1. His first question, upon being introduced to you, is whether you are a U.S. citizen.
2. He proposes marriage on the first date.
3. His favorite movie is *Green Card*.
4. His excuse for forgetting your name is that he prefers to call you "dear one" in his native language.
5. He puts on dark glasses when you walk by any government offices.
6. He pleads with you to introduce his two brothers to your two sisters.
7. He proposes marriage on the second date.

▼▼

◉ When You're Neither Dazzled Nor Deadened

If you have mixed feelings about whether you want to see the man again, or if you were bored for only part of the evening, go for it. Give the man a second chance. Perhaps he felt nervous or awkward, and will be more at ease on a second date. Perhaps he had just finished a difficult day at work when you met. Or maybe he was thrown off track by the fact that you look so much like his ex-girlfriend—and there was no way you'd know that. Try again. Plan a different sort of date to see if you find him more appealing in a different setting. If you're undecided, get a second opinion from an encouraging friend. Explain the pros and cons, the highs (if any) and lows of the evening, and see what she says.

Lots of second dates are better than the first ones. Be open. You can always say no later.

▲▲▲

Male Voices III

Howard, a Los Angeles screenwriter: "Be straight with me. That's all I ask."

Glenn, an Atlanta business consultant: "Spare me the details of your last visit to your therapist on the first date."

Jim, a New York writer: "Women should understand and appreciate that it's not at all easy for men to make that first call and ask them for a date. The fear of rejection is pretty high."

Jerry, a New Jersey teacher: "I meet most of the women I date at parties. It's easier for me to approach a woman who's alone than one who hangs out with her girlfriends all night."

Jack, a Chicago businessman: "Chivalry lives. I like to open doors, pay for my date (at least the first few times)."

Eliot, a Cleveland journalist: "I've placed ads that have gotten lots and varied responses. The ones I call back first are those that somehow sound honest and not clichéd."

Ben, a Florida attorney: "Men are pretty simple people. Women needn't think so much about all of this."

▼▼▼

A Special Note on the Second Time Around

A season is set for everything, a time for every experience under heaven.
                              —Ecclesiastes 3:1

No one has ever measured, even poets, how much a heart can hold.
                              —Zelda Fitzgerald

*Y*ou didn't think you'd ever have to be doing this again.
   You thought your last partner was for life. You hadn't given much thought to dating; it was something other women did. But through one of life's unexpected twists, you're on your own again.
   If you're even reading this book, you must be ready—or al-

most there—to consider going out with men again. Take your time; it's fine to enter the world of dating as slowly as you're comfortable. The pace you set is your own—there's no need to follow anyone else's timetable.

If you can't remember the last time you even went on a date with someone you didn't know, or if you feel your skills in this area are rusty, it might take a little while to get your bearings again. Try to go out on a few dates—even if you'd rather spend your time doing *anything* else—just for the sake of experience. You might be surprised at how much you enjoy the companionship as well as the attention; it's kind of fun to feel like a teenager again.

Don't worry if you're nowhere near ready to think about marrying (many men aren't either), or if you value your newly gained independence too much to think about giving it up again. Your goal in dating might be simply to find a few comfortable relationships, some kind men as occasional dinner or movie companions, or someone intriguing for a grand fling.

It's Never Too Late

Advice columnist Ann Landers, who has been divorced for twenty-one years after a thirty-six-year marriage, has a very active social life at age seventy-six. She told a reporter that she loves her life-style and does not want to get married again. The woman who has been advising Americans on love and other matters for thirty-nine years met her "gentleman friend" at a Washington dinner party. Although they were each there with another date, they mainly talked with each other. When he asked her if she visited Washington frequently, she said, "I'll get here more often, believe me." And she does.

☀ A Reintroduction to Dating in the '90s

Life might be different from the last time you dated. Feminism. Robert Bly and the men's movement. AIDS, herpes, vending machines with condoms. Date rape on campus. Escalating divorce rates, royal divorces too. Blended families, custody battles. Postponed childbirth, surrogate mothers, bombings of abortion clinics. Recession. Jane Fonda and Ted Turner.

Perhaps you identify with the classic *Peanuts* cartoon, in which Snoopy announces something to the effect that when he learned all the answers, they changed all the questions.

Don't worry that the rules of dating have changed and you no longer know what they are. In fact, there are no rules. Just be cautious (yes, you can be cautious *and* open). And it's never a bad idea to remember to treat others as you'd like to be treated.

▲▲▲

Conversation Savers (What to Discuss When Silence Is Deadly)

1. The latest James Bond/Liv Ullmann/Steven Spielberg film—take your pick.
2. The conversation at the next table.
3. Those Cubs/Mets/Lakers.
4. Your most dramatic "kindness of strangers" story.
5. The latest gruesome murder story, political scandal, latest best-selling novel (you need not have read it) everyone is talking about.
6. Questions: Ask anything—Most people never tire of talking about themselves.
7. The weather.

▼▼▼

As you think about dating again, let your friends, particularly those who are themselves dating, know that you are ready. Ask them to share their experiences (most women are more than pleased to oblige), and their impressions of the "world out there." Question them about your concerns. It's very important not to be turned off by one person's bad experience or bad luck. You might have a stroke of that too, but better times will certainly follow. Dating isn't always easy, but it's worthwhile. Here's some grandmotherly wisdom on the subject: It takes time, but it only takes one.

Find someone you trust and enjoy sharing your dating stories with. Review your adventures in as much detail as you're comfortable. Have a partner, or several, to giggle with the day after. It helps to bounce your feelings and reactions off caring friends, whether male or female. They'll help keep you on track.

Who to Go Out With

You're a perfect candidate to be "matched." Let your friends, colleagues at work, and relatives (see Chapter 3 for additional ideas) know that you're ready to date again and that you'd really appreciate their introducing you to any single men they know and like. If you have in mind a specific person whom a friend knows, ask your friend to make the introduction. Remember, you're helping your friend do a favor for his or her friend.

You should also think about old friends. Keep abreast of what's going on in their lives. Your college boyfriends or former colleagues may be in a similar situation to yours. They too might be on their second—or third or fourth—time around. You can also think about men you knew while they were married, who are newly single after death or divorce. Call them. They're likely to be delighted to hear from you. Or have a mutual friend call on your behalf. Be cautious about timing: You want to contact him before many others have the same idea, but do give him time to adjust to his new situation. You may not find romance but you may find another new friend who's had an experience similar to yours.

See chapters 4 and 5 for good advice on places to meet new interesting men. You might think of joining groups geared to your age group. Try different options—placing ads, answering ads, taking classes, volunteering—and see what's most comfortable for you. Practice being open.

▲▲▲
It Is Okay to Let Your Date Know
1. The following day is your birthday.
2. You're allergic to the Mexican food he plans to serve you.
3. You noticed him the first day of class and you're really pleased that he called.
4. You've never met the friend of your aunt who is responsible for introducing you.
5. You think that his shirt and tie are magnificent.
6. Although he's forgotten, you're the person who . . .
7. This is the first blind date you've ever agreed to.
▼▼

For Single Mothers: Dating With Kids

If a friend introduces you to someone, you can assume your date knows you're a single mother. When you go out with a new man you've met on your own, it's best to be up front about your children. There's no way to keep facts like that hidden for long, and you wouldn't want to. For many single mothers, the most important quality in a man can be his love of children.

A potentially more sensitive issue than telling your date about your kids is talking to your kids about dating. If they're young, you'll also need to address the issue of how soon you introduce them to your dates. A wise friend advises letting your kids know that you are dating, and, depending on their age and personalities, telling them about specific people you meet. However, she suggests introducing them only to a man you might feel seriously about. That way, kids are shielded from the ups and downs of dating, which at any age might be hard for them to handle. The same holds true for introducing them to his kids.

When you decide the time is right to bring together your kids and a man you are seeing, plan the meeting in a comfortable setting. You might want to plan an outing or an activity that everyone—especially the kids—will enjoy. If the kids are young, a trip to the zoo or a museum might work well. The more distractions, the better. A sit-down get-acquainted meal can be quite stressful, so save it for a subsequent meeting.

If he has his own set of kids, you may want to bring everyone together after, separately, you've met his kids, and he's met yours. By nature, such meetings are complicated and tense but also full of wonderful potential. Think of *The Brady Bunch*. Again, plan an activity—full of diversions—of interest to all. Try to be relaxed about the whole thing; although you can do your best to make it easy for everyone, you can't guarantee that all involved will like each other or the situation.

Of course, you'll want to navigate this new landscape with great care. However, while you're being sensitive to your kids' needs, be certain not to sacrifice your own.

Talking About Your Past

When it comes to dating, the past comes up in (at least) two ways: (1) Letting the ghosts out: sharing stories of past loves, and (2) The ghost as guest: referring to an ex or deceased spouse or lover with such frequency that he seems to be a third party to the conversation. The first is healthy and often a source of camaraderie with a date; the second is to be avoided if you are interested in a second date.

How soon to talk about a former husband? As soon as you feel comfortable. Divorced people who date other divorced people are likely to speak of their previous marriages as early as the first date, at least in broad strokes. Some people find that telling the marital equivalent of war stories can provide common ground, and that the process itself is almost therapeutic. And, you can learn a lot about a man and his values from the way he speaks of a failed marriage. A divorced woman who dates frequently says that she prefers meeting men who are also divorced because she can usually speak quite openly with them, and "avoid a lot of small talk" on the way to getting to know them.

If you find yourself speaking frequently about your former husband, you might want to rethink your approach, and also reconsider if you are really ready to date yet. You might need to take some additional time for healing.

While drawing comparisons between people is a natural instinct, try not to measure each man you meet by how well he stands up to the last man you were with. Those sorts of judgments will prevent you from getting to know the person and perhaps realizing that your quick analysis was off base. Be open. I hope you'll be wonderfully surprised.

Overdating

Too Many Men

Hope is the feeling you have that the feeling you have isn't permanent.
—Jean Kerr

The heart is a very resilient little muscle.
—Micky, in Woody Allen's
Crimes and Misdemeanors

Too many dates: The problem you'd wished for. You never thought you'd need advice on how to stop meeting smart men.

Marathon dating: You can't remember which of your jokes you've told to which man. You're not certain if you saw the movie you're about to mention with the man sitting across from you or with another. You don't recall if you introduced the man you think you like best, or the second runner-up, to your best friend. You've had the same conversation so many times that you find yourself talking without really paying attention to what you're saying. You're not even sure who sent you the flowers. You're not even sure you care.

Sometimes life feels like the reruns of a situation comedy you vaguely remember. All this attention might delight you as nothing has since your moment of glorious popularity in the sixth grade—or it might cause more angst than you care to experience, thank you very much.

If having an overbooked dance card delights or amuses you, enjoy every minute. Just try to keep the names straight. You might keep a record of where you've been and who you went with in your calendar for easy reference when one of your dates leaves a message inviting you to dinner at his favorite restaurant—you know, the one you went to on your first date.

If, on the other hand, you're feeling overwhelmed and ready to ditch all of your suitors, don't—at least, not yet. Slow down and simplify. Select those you're most interested in and gently let go of the others. Limit your schedule to one or two dates per week; plan a dateless weekend. Share the wealth with other unattached women you know.

▲▲

Sure-fire Signs of Dating Burnout

1. You fast-forward your VCR when you get to the dating scenes in old movies.
2. Your recurring dream is that the five men you've been dating arrive at your home at once.
3. You can't stop humming the song from *South Pacific* "I'm gonna wash that man right out of my hair."
4. You start wearing your mother's engagement ring and wedding band.
5. You wrote "not interested" on a credit card slip that asked for your name and date.

▼▼

However, if one more date is still too many, and if you don't care for anyone you've met on this whirlwind of blind dates and are sickened by the thought of ever going on a d-a-t-e again, you may have a simple—and curable—case of dating burnout. You've moved quickly from the how-tos of dating to the how-do-I-get-out-of-this blues. Don't worry, it will pass. But meanwhile you need to be refreshed.

 ## Curing the One-Date-Too-Many Blues

Give yourself a complete respite from dating. Declare a moratorium on having coffee with strangers. Stay away from singles events. If someone calls to ask you to go out with him, say that you'd like to but are busy for the next short while and will call him back. (Hold on to the number.) Spend some free time with married friends. Baby-sit for their kids. Read Mother Teresa's memoirs. Organize your closets. Take a weekend trip with a friend. Don't even glance at the personals. Try a creative visualization. Think of a couple you know who seem very happy together, and imagine how you would feel in a similar situation.

You'll know you're cured and ready to give your telephone number to your cousin again when you begin scanning crowds for a man who might be looking for you. Unconsciously, you'll start humming "The Look of Love." Perhaps you'll find yourself again daydreaming about romantic dinners and conversations you don't want to end. Slowly, you'll stop screening your phone calls and pretending to be your sister when you do pick up and hear a man's voice. Soon, you might feel awfully curious about the man (no ring) sitting next to you on the plane. Go on, flirt with dignity.

13

Last Dates? Last Words

We love being in love, that's the truth on't.
    —William Makepeace Thackeray

Trust thyself: every heart vibrates to that iron string.
    —Ralph Waldo Emerson

By now, you may have lots of smart men in your life. Enjoy them; enjoy yourself.

But, if after 129 pages of coaching, you still feel shy about approaching new men, don't let that stop you from trying. Keep at it. Take risks. You're bound to feel better with more practice and experience. Even if you've tried going to bookstores and joining organizations, have friends and relatives on full alert for matchmaking opportunities, and your best efforts have yet to yield success, keep trying. Each encounter, every experience, brings you closer to finding what you seek.

Most of all, don't lose heart. Good fortune can't be far away; remember that it's all about timing. You might be doing everything just right. Be patient. Add something new to your repertoire: Take out a personal ad; sign up for sailing lessons; find an outdoor café you love sitting at; look up your still-single high school sweetheart. Keep your heart open. Don't ever forget that you're great company.

Remember the Eleventh Hour Syndrome. It's highly likely that you'll meet a great man just as you're ready to exit. Several friends tell me that in summer camp they would find boyfriends on one of the last nights of the summer. It's not unusual for women to meet men as their vacations are ending, on the last day of class, or while getting their coats at a party. In those final moments, when your guard is down, when you feel most relaxed, when you least expect it, don't be surprised if you meet a terrific man—or two.

The End of Dating?

You may discover that things are going so well that you don't want to stop dating, that going out with several men while also meeting new ones is preferable to a singular relationship. Perhaps you're having a fabulous time and delighting in the plural attention. Sounds great, if it suits you—and it suits many.

Keep in mind that dating is one of those skills that its best practitioners can grow out of, or lose the need to practice what they've learned. It's not unlike learning to crawl. Soon after toddlers become masters at crawling, they pick themselves up and walk. They'll never forget how to crawl, but they'll have less use for the talent. So too with dating. When you reach your peak in expertise (or even before)—when you continuously meet appealing and datable men—you just might give it up. You'll have made the leap from meeting men as smart as you to finding the one man smart enough for you.

Back to crawling for a moment. Long after you've learned to rely on walking upright, you might find yourself on all fours again, searching for a contact lens, or playing with a child. Yes, after you've graduated with honors from the How to Meet Men as Smart as You School of Dating, and think that finally you've gone on your last date, you might find yourself in a situation where you want to begin meeting interesting men to date, again. Once you've developed dating prowess, you won't lose it. Moreover, the new outlook you've developed—being friendly and approachable in all situations, being open to the unexpected—is a boost for life.

✓ Questions You'll Have to Answer for Yourself

Perhaps you've found a man as smart as you. Should you keep dating him? Should you marry him? What if he's nice but not quite the man of your dreams? How do you know when it's time to stop dating someone you feel at best mildly interested in? What if you want to take it slow and he's in a hurry? Or vice versa? What qualities are most important? Can you really date more than one man at a time? Is it okay to choose continued dating over settling down? What does it take to make a relationship really work?

Those questions of the heart can't be answered within the pages of any book. My hope is to provide you with new ideas—to show you how to find your own successful approach—to get to the very nice place in life where you're asking some of these questions.

Dating is by nature perplexing, and a certain confusion is inevitable. Share your thoughts and fears with friends who know and love you well, or seek insight from a professional counselor. You might enjoy browsing through the many self-help books published about relationships, and you're likely to find helpful information but, ultimately, your story—and your questions—are your own. Take long walks; read poetry; watch old movies; treat yourself to a Swedish massage. Search your heart. And good luck.

Still Splendidly Single

And if you don't meet a man you care about on this round of dating, that's fine too. Go on enjoying your life. Pursue your many interests. Your life is no less full—only different—without a boyfriend or husband. A young fiftysomething friend who has never been married and works as a tour guide wouldn't trade her singlehood for any marriage. She has friends (and boyfriends) in the many places she travels, and she savors her independence and freedom.

You decide. Go out as much as you like; marry or not. Live well. Yes, be open and flexible and wise. May you have many smart dates who appreciate how savvy and splendid you are.

Acknowledgments

Call it a clan, call it a network, call it a tribe.
Whatever you call it, whoever you are, you need
one.

　　　　　　　　—Jane Howard

$\mathcal{M}$y first experiences with dating were vicarious. Not only did I watch my older sisters, Phyllis Brawarsky and Diane Brawarsky, prepare for their dates but I'd make sure to overhear their conversations afterward. Sometimes, they'd have to take me along and I, no doubt, enjoyed those evenings more than they did. One suitor—now my brother-in-law William—impressed me most by giving me a ride on the back of his motorcycle. I thank them for the introduction to dating, and my brother-in-law Noah, too, for sharing their stories and their love.

And I thank my parents. No match is perfect—as I tell people I'm about to fix up—but theirs is close. I owe my matchmaking inspiration to my father. Although my track record is more impressive than his, he keeps trying.

Many thanks to the friends who told me their tales of dating, tested out my advice, and allowed me to try out my matchmaking hunches on them. I'm grateful to Denise Berthiaume, Judy Epstein, Nancy Miller, Bill Parkhurst, and, especially, Deborah Brodie, for their wise comments and counsel on the manuscript. My nieces Erica DeVos, Sarah DeVos, Marnina Cherkin, and Emily Cherkin helped by offering the perspective of women younger than I.

I'm indebted to this book's matchmaker, my literary agent and friend, Carla Glasser. She had the idea—a brilliant one, I think—to introduce me to my editor, Sheila Curry, with whom it has been a pleasure to work. I appreciate her many efforts and those of her colleagues at Fireside.

And, finally, special thanks to Lester Gottesman. Yes, I've met one very smart man.

▲▲

You must have your own tried-and-true theories about dating, as well as some great best date/worst date stories. I'd love to hear from you about what works and what doesn't, your tales of dates from heaven as well as hell, and any advice you can share with other women seeking to meet interesting men. Please address your correspondence to Sandee Brawarsky, c/o Fireside Books, 1230 Sixth Avenue, New York, New York 10020. I welcome your letters. There's much we can learn from each other.

▼▼

Index

accountants, 33, 39, 108
acquaintances, 20, 23–24
activities, 39–40, 46–54
    best, 46–54
    frequent participation in, 40, 44
    group, 49–53, 74, 79, 99
    "male," 40
    singles', 47, 50, 59, 63–64
age, 12, 37, 65, 116, 121
AIDS, 122
airports, 61, 104
Alaska Men, 78
Allen, Woody, 22, 127
alumni events, 54–55, 78
Angelou, Maya, 98
apartments, 20, 32, 35, 106
architects, 33
art:
    exhibitions of, 41, 42
    shared interest in, 22, 41, 65
Ask Any Girl (Wolfe), 93
As You Like It (Shakespeare), 38, 86
attitude, 14–16, 130–31
    openness of, 14, 27–28, 29,
        39–40, 59, 80–85, 94, 131
auctions, 41
Austen, Jane, 98

babies, 15, 28–29
Bachelor Book, 78
backgrounds, 21, 22, 32, 116
Baker, James, 26
bars, 41, 43–44, 58, 102–3
bartenders, 44, 82
Beyond Therapy (Durang), 68
Bible, 17, 120
bicycling, 42, 78, 104
biographical profiles, 65, 66, 67,
    68, 71–72, 76

Bly, Robert, 122
boat rides, 64, 104
body language, 83, 100
books, 16, 44, 115, 132–33
    carrying of, 61, 81, 82
    discussions and readings of, 44,
        46–47, 50, 81
bookstores, 44, 46, 50, 52, 84
Brides, 12
bridge, 20, 21, 74
browsing, 42, 44, 52, 84, 132
brunches, 59, 64
bulletin boards, 50, 74
buses, 40, 53, 61, 81, 104
business cards, 9, 40, 63, 84, 94, 95,
    96
business conferences, 77, 95

cafés, 15, 41, 43, 44, 56, 75, 77, 82,
    102
camaraderie, 18
carpools, 36
Carville, James, 60
Cemetery Club, The, 28
charm, 82, 83
children, 20, 28–29, 36, 52, 54, 83,
    116, 124–25
    activities for, 77–78, 125
choirs, 47
classes, 39, 48–49, 53, 81, 84
class reunions, 54–55, 78
clergy, 32, 47, 78
Club Med, 53–54
cocktail parties, 59, 82
coffee dates, 15, 30, 43, 62, 73, 84,
    95, 96, 103
colleagues, 20, 23, 27, 33, 59–60, 123
college reunions, 55
committee meetings, 36, 49, 50

community organizations, 36, 46, 48, 49–50, 53
computers, 43, 69, 75
  networking with, 13, 74–75
concerts, 24, 42, 81, 96, 103
continuing education, 48–49
control, staying in, 26–27, 30, 99–102
conversations:
  common ground in, 40, 81
  following through in, 45, 47, 83–84, 94
  initiation of, 13, 14, 24, 40–47, 54, 56, 61–62, 77–78, 80–82, 83, 91
  interruption of, 21
  lulls in, 82, 83, 100, 122
  on-line, 13, 74–75
  pretexts for, 14, 40, 41, 43, 54, 81, 91
  receptiveness to, 81–83, 90–94
  subjects to avoid in, 107, 125
  subjects to broach in, 122, 124
  teamwork in, 83–84
  techniques of, 83–84, 90–93
  see also telephone calls
Conversations With My Father (Gardner), 11
couples, 21
  age differences in, 37, 65
  chemistry of, 87
  complementary qualities in, 22, 23
  mismatched, 19–20, 32
  reconnection of, 20
  shared values and interests of, 18, 22, 40, 41, 60, 65–66, 81, 90, 103
crafts fairs, 42, 79
Crimes and Misdemeanors, 22, 127
Crossing Delancey, 28, 30
cultural institutions, 46, 52

dancing, 51–52, 63
dates:
  accidental repeat of, 33

arrangement of, 13, 17, 18, 20–25, 30–32, 63, 69, 76, 84, 90–97, 99–104
blind, 13, 18, 30–32, 33, 37, 59, 63, 90–94, 109
changing mores of, 122
curtailing of, 109
dealing with predicaments on, 110–11
decision making on, 99–102
double, 111
dressing for, 105
endings of, 111–12
extension of, 31
financial arrangements on, 107–8
first, 13, 15, 18, 20, 30–31, 69, 73, 98–112
group, 31, 74
mail-order, 78
overbooking of, 13, 127–29
post-divorce, 13, 28, 67, 120–21, 126
post-event discussions of, 20, 31, 109
precautions with, 92, 99, 122
readiness for, 14–15, 24, 27
rejection of, 92
second, 25, 114
setting agendas for, 26, 27, 30, 99–102
strangers' requests for, 14, 90–93
women's requests for, 94–97, 101
Dating Game, The, 76
dating services, 63
day trips, 53, 74
decision making, 26, 27, 99–102
Defending Your Life, 28
destiny, 12–13, 38–39
dining clubs, 64
dinner dates, 14, 31, 33, 79, 95, 103
dinner parties, 24, 31, 47, 79, 101–2, 121
discussion groups, 47, 50

divorce, 122, 123–24
  dating after, 13, 28, 67, 120–21, 126
doctors, 42, 79
dog walking, 77
Dostoevski, Fyodor, 89
Dumas, Alexandre, 113
Durang, Christopher, 68

Ehrenreich, Barbara, 58
Eliezer, 17
Emerson, Ralph Waldo, 130
encounters:
  chance, 13, 14, 38–39, 61–62
  curiosity and, 14
  first, 13, 38–39
  frequent, 40, 44, 47, 84
  precautions with, 62
  strategies for, 38–57, 77–79
Ephron, Nora, 72
events, 54–57
  arrival and departure at, 56
  best, 54–56
  group, 31, 56–57
  information about, 46, 63
  singles-only, 63–64, 100
exercise, 42, 44–45, 51, 77
eye contact, 62, 81–83

fax dates, 13, 97
feminism, 122
festivals, 42
Fiddler on the Roof (Bock and Harnick), 18, 19
financial advisors, 16, 60
financial status, 116
first impressions, 48
Fitzgerald, Zelda, 120
flirting, 28, 49, 82–83
"frequent sightings" principle, 40, 44
friends:
  activities with, 16, 56–57, 83–84
  advice from, 13, 72, 91
  assistance of, 13, 27–28, 30–32, 76, 83–84, 123

male, 20, 28, 59, 86–88, 108–109
  matchmaking by, 13, 19, 20–25, 27, 30–32, 36, 62, 82
  "rescue" by, 84
  reunions with, 54–55, 62, 78
  romantic developments with, 28, 86–88
  scrutiny of, 31
  special arrangements with, 57, 83–84
  telephone, 60–61
fund-raising, 49–50, 79, 90

galleries, 41, 84, 103
gardens, 42, 103
Gardner, Herb, 11
Gordon, Ruth, 25

hairdressers, 34
handwriting, 69, 73
Hawn, Goldie, 95
health, 116
health clubs, 44–45, 53
Heidi Chronicles, The (Wasserstein), 48
Hello, Dolly! (Herman), 25
high school reunions, 54–55
hiking, 53, 64
Holmes, Oliver Wendell, 17
hospitals, 79
hotels, 15, 103
Howard, Jane, 135
Husbands and Wives, 28

Ideal Husband, An (Wilde), 89
index cards, 21
interests:
  data on, 21, 65–66
  male, 40
  mutual, 22, 40, 41, 60, 65–66, 81, 90, 103
  pursuing of, 40, 48–52, 64
interior designers, 33
introductions, 44, 57
  asking for, 25, 31, 35

introductions *(cont.)*
  matchmaking, 15, 17, 18, 20–25,
    31
  openness to, 22–24
  self, 39, 54
Isn't It Romantic (Wasserstein), 39

Jewett, Sarah Orne, 30
jobs, 20, 26–27, 67
  working together and, 38, 59–60
jury duty, 13, 55–56

Kerr, Jean, 127

Landers, Ann, 121
language study, 53
Lardner, Ring, 58
laundromats, 77
lawyers, 33, 60
lectures, public, 46, 47, 80, 103
letter carriers, 35
Letterman, David, 72
letters, 65–69, 75, 78–79, 115
libraries, 42–43, 46
lifestyles, 22
lines, waiting on, 43, 52, 56, 81
Little League, 78, 104
Loftus, Tom, 26–27
Loos, Anita, 38
Los Angeles, 70
love, 11, 13, 16, 17, 18
Love at First Sight, 76
Love Connection, 76
lunch dates, 60, 63

Mabley, Jackie "Moms," 17
magazines, 44, 61, 70, 75, 81
manners, 100, 101, 108, 109
marriage:
  arranged, 11
  citizenship and, 118
  clues to status of, 21, 114, 116
  contemplation of, 15, 121
  matchmaking resulting in, 9, 15,
    17, 18, 21, 24, 25

  previous, 13, 28, 67, 116, 120–21
  statistics on, 12, 37
marriage brokers, 62–63
Matalin, Mary, 60
Matchmaker, The (Wilder), 25
matchmaking, 17–25
  appreciation of, 32, 34, 109
  biblical, 17
  business aspects of, 11, 18, 19, 20
  collaborative, 23–24, 62
  difficulties of, 18, 19–20, 23–24
  discretion and restraint in, 20,
    24, 32, 35
  ethnic traditions of, 17–19, 62–63
  faith and trust in, 24
  by friends, 13, 19, 20–25, 27,
    30–32, 36, 62, 82
  full disclosure and, 19, 22–23,
    27–28
  intuition in, 22, 31
  marital outcome of, 9, 15, 17, 18,
    21, 24, 25
  methodology and manners of,
    20–23, 30–32, 36
  motives for, 18–19, 25
  non-romantic, 20
  professional, 17–18, 62–63
  self, 25
  skills of, 18–24, 92
  stereotypes of, 9, 18
  television, 76
matrimonial services, 62–63
meditation, 16
men's movement, 122
mnemonic devices, 85
movies, 56, 100, 101, 103, 104
Much Ado About Nothing (Shake-
    speare), 80
museums, 41, 46, 49, 53, 56, 64, 99,
    101
negotiation, 11, 27, 28–29
neighbors, 36, 39
networking, 26, 27–28, 31–36, 135
  computer, 13, 74–75
  resources for, 32–36, 65–66

newsletters, singles, 65–66
newsstands, 44
New York Review of Books, The, 70
New York Times, The, 35, 55
night court, 103

O'Brien, Glenn, 95
office romances, 59–60
"One Tooth and Two Tooth," 79

parents, 19, 20, 59
   advice from, 39, 57
   single, 36, 52, 54, 77–78, 124–25
parks, 42, 77–78, 103
parties, 24, 38, 63, 94, 119
   introductions at, 24, 85
   overcoming shyness at, 85
   ratio of men to women at, 59
Peanuts, 122
personal ads, 13, 50, 65–74, 92
   arranged meetings and, 69, 73,
      99
   biographical profiles in, 65, 66,
      67, 68, 71–72
   code system in, 67
   cost of, 66, 70
   following up on responses to, 73
   group, 74
   photographs and, 70
   placing of, 66, 70–72
   precautions with, 68
   reevaluation of, 73–74
   responding to, 66, 67–69
   selecting publications for, 70, 74
   voice-mail systems and, 66–67,
      69
   wording of, 71–72
personal trainers, 45
Philadelphia, 70
physical appearance, 39, 61, 71, 75,
   100
Playboy, 95
political campaigns, 49, 60
prayer, 47, 79
Private Benjamin, 95

public places, 39, 42, 56, 62, 69, 99
punctuality, 99

questions, 28, 79, 83, 122
   getting-acquainted, 14, 15, 21,
      90, 99, 116
   of self, 132–33
   starting conversations with, 14,
      41, 44, 54, 81, 85

rape, 122
readings, 46–47, 81
real estate agents, 32
rejection, fear of, 119
relatives, 15, 23, 123
   matchmaking by, 19, 23, 24, 27,
      36, 62, 90
religion, 32, 62, 79, 116
religious services, 36, 47
religious sites, 79
relocation, 32, 33, 35, 58
restaurants, 15, 35, 64, 68, 82, 99,
   102–3, 104
   noise in, 100, 102
   ordering in, 108
   price range of, 103
roommates, 20, 27
Rubin, Louis, 18
Rudner, Rita, 113

sailing, 36, 51, 131
salespeople, 34, 61
school committees, 49
schoolmates, 38, 54–55, 62
seating arrangements, 24, 46, 47,
   48, 61, 83
self-esteem, 82
sense of humor, 14
Sergel, Christopher, 93
sex, 76, 111, 122
Shakespeare, William, 38, 80, 86
Sharman, Helen, 26
shopping, 39, 40, 44, 52, 103
shyness, 82, 85
Simon, Neil, 39

single state:
    activities for, 47, 50, 63–66
    benefits of, 15, 16, 133
    clues to, 21
    returning to, 32
Six Degrees of Separation (Guare),
    32
skiing, 51, 63, 80
Sleepless in Seattle, 28, 72
Smiley, Jane, 86
sports:
    coaching of, 49
    matching partners for, 20, 21,
        27, 50–51, 82
    noncompetitive, 104
    spectator, 51, 101, 104
    see also exercise; *specific sports*
sports clubs, 51, 56
Star-Spangled Girl, The (Simon), 39
Stein, Joseph, 19
Studs, 76
summer houses, 32, 79

tailors, 34
taxi drivers, 78
teachers, 27, 34, 41, 48–49, 51
telephone calls, 35, 60–61
    answering machines and, 67,
        89–90, 95
    discouragement of, 117–18
    first contact by, 89–97
    promises of, 22–23, 113–14, 115
    responding to personal ads with,
        66–67, 73
    returning of, 13, 14, 67
    setting up of, 22–23, 30, 33
    screening of, 90
    by women, 73, 94–96, 115
    at work, 62, 92
    wrong number, 60
telephone numbers, 60, 82, 90, 95,
    96
tennis, 20, 21, 27, 50–51, 63, 82, 104

Thackeray, William Makepeace,
    130
theater, 42, 51, 64, 78
timing, 12, 38–39, 60, 114–15,
    123–24
tours, 49, 53, 103
trains, 61, 81
travel, 61–62, 77, 81, 104

universities, 42, 46, 55
ushering, 78

vacations, 53–54, 62, 94, 131
    group, 53
    planning of, 16, 53–54
    solo, 13, 53, 54
valentines, 83
video dating, 75–76
visualization, 86, 106
voices, 22, 37, 60, 61, 68, 89–90
volunteer work, 49–50

waiters, 35, 82, 100
walking, 42, 101
Wall Street Journal, The, 17–18, 74
Wasserstein, Wendy, 39, 48
wedding rings, 21, 114
weddings, 51
    attendance at, 23, 52
    matchmaking at, 9, 22, 38, 54
    "on line," 75
    planning of, 54
When Harry Met Sally, 28, 87
Wilde, Oscar, 89
Wilder, Thornton, 25
wine-tasting, 78
Wolfe, Winifred, 93
writers, 46–47, 60, 78

Yente, 18, 19
youth groups, 49

zoos, 103